IMAGES
of America

BAKER ISLAND

On the Cover: No known photographs exist of the original 1828 lighthouse; this c. 1869 image shows its 1855 replacement, inhabited by the Bunkers. The dark board-and-batten keeper's house, pictured without ell or dormers, was whitewashed in 1879. On the southeast corner is not the c. 1870 ell, but a kitchen. Dormers were added between 1898 and 1905. The privy is visible behind and to the left. (National Archives and Records Administration.)

Cornelia J. Cesari

ISBN 978-1-4671-2912-1

Published by Arcadia Publishing
Charleston, South Carolina

Printed in the United States of America

Library of Congress Control Number: 2017962382

For all general information, please contact Arcadia Publishing:
Telephone 843-853-2070
Fax 843-853-0044
E-mail sales@arcadiapublishing.com
For customer service and orders:
Toll-Free 1-888-313-2665

Visit us on the Internet at www.arcadiapublishing.com

To Baker residents Ronald and Kathleen Pearson, Henry and Elizabeth Kolm, their progeny, and sons-in-law who are dedicated to a new era of stewardship. And to Phebe Jane, Leona, the Hats, and the Hannahs—stalwart Baker matriarchs whose spirits are omnipresent.

Contents

ACKNOWLEDGMENTS

Much has been written about Baker Island, with varying accuracy but always with passion. I wanted to compile a long-awaited comprehensive, accurate history, basing my research upon material as close to primary sources as practicable. The work was endless and endlessly fascinating; I hope this volume elicits more contributions to the historical record of Baker Island for decades to come.

Recognition and deep gratitude go to a few tireless individuals and organizations who have been especially generous with time and resources. Documenting and preserving lighthouse history are Candace Clifford (Lighthouse Society), Tim Harrison and Debra Baldwin (*Lighthouse Digest*), and Kraig Anderson (Lighthouse Friends). Historical societies on Islesford and Great Cranberry Island offered assistance and access, as did folks at the Maine State Archives and National Park Service Longfellow House–Washington's Headquarters.

With gratitude to over a dozen local historical societies, libraries, and archives, all playing vital roles in their communities, I applaud the mission of Mount Desert Island Historical Society of preservation, collaboration, and open access. I believe that history belongs to all, and while time and labor deserve remuneration, this is no place for pettiness or proprietary possessiveness. Arcadia Publishing's model furthers this philosophy.

The incomparable Ralph W. Stanley shared his family history, photographs, and letters. Relatives and descendants of teachers, Gilleys, lighthouse keepers, and rusticators received my peculiar requests (to paw through their family albums) with grace and even gusto. I hope I have adequately honored their forebears whose stories are woven into the tapestry of Baker Island.

A few specific mentions are warranted. The support and generosity of Henry and Gail Grandgent, the Sawyer family, Gail Carr, and Mildred Chalmers were indispensable in the production of this book. Fellow residents of the Cranberry Isles have greeted us across the bar for decades. At Acadia National Park, many individuals have demonstrated commitment to Baker and are greatly appreciated but too numerous to name. Interpretive rangers guide thousands with enthusiasm and respect, fire management personnel have been inspiring on-the-ground partners, and personnel in resource management and enforcement work to protect and maintain Baker Island within complex procedural considerations and financial constraints.

Finally, I have no words to thank my best friend, partner, and husband, John, whose vision, perseverance, and countless hours of unpaid, unpublicized hard work have transformed Baker Island.

The images in this volume appear courtesy of Acadia National Park Archives (ANP), Southwest Harbor Public Library Archives (SWHPL), National Archives and Records Administration (NARA), United States Coast Guard (USCG), Maine Historic Preservation Commission (MHPC), *Lighthouse Digest* (LHD), Lighthouse Friends (LHF), Northeast Harbor Public Library (NEHPL), Seal Harbor Public Library (SHPL), Great Harbor Maritime Museum (GHMM), Islesford Historical Society (IHS), Great Cranberry Island Historical Society (GCIHS), Keepers of Baker Island (KOBI), and individuals credited in the captions.

Introduction

First things first. The two most frequently asked questions are: is it Baker's or Baker, and why "Baker" anyway? Baker's shows up in a 1760s map of land grants, but the name changed officially to Baker at some point between 1887 and 1891.

Why Baker? No one knows, but there are three common theories: first, it is shaped like a cake; second, it is similar to the earlier Baker's Island in Massachusetts; and third, Nellie Carroll Thornton's *Traditions and Records of Southwest Harbor and Somesville* (1938) references a William Baker, who shows up in the 1760 census, and also a certain "Grandma'am Baker," who was summoned in times of sickness before Dr. Kittredge's practice started in 1799. "Stories are told of times when men turned out in numbers to get Grandma'am Baker to the house of suffering; sometimes to the adjoining islands across turbulent seas or through floating ice, through drifting snows or driving rains," Thornton wrote. "The old lady was often carried on a hand-barrow by men when the call was from a distance or over rough roads." Were they bringing her from Baker's Island?

Baker Island is a secret. My secret.

These are the feelings, if not the actual words, of an astonishing number of people. One wants to share this magical place with the world, and yet one does not want to let the word get out. To me, this is an example of one way in which Baker is a place of contradictions. It is universal and yet unique, a shared experience while intensely private.

Visiting is marvelous in the present, as I trust it will be in the future. But the past—Baker Island oozes history like a saturated clump of moss. Walking up the path, standing by the lighthouse, watching a sunset—every experience is akin to climbing a staircase in an old house and pondering the hands that have trailed the satin-smooth banister before yours.

Many lives have intersected on this tiny island. Single time visitors and Phebe Jane Stanley (who spent 87 years here, without leaving for the last 36) all admired the stunning Acadia skyline. In 1914, teacher Sara Mayo described that same skyline to her mother back home—as did recruit Lyle Stepanek 30 years later, just months before a torpedo ended his life in the North Atlantic. The Muise children—two brothers and a sister the same ages as my children—were building a raft 70 years before mine were when Ronald Muise drowned. The only connection? Baker Island.

The process of writing this book has taken me all over the country, physically and electronically. I have followed leads to long-forgotten war casualties, scandal, and intrigue. I have called strangers out of the blue and asked to show up on their doorsteps with my scanner and paw through their attics. I have introduced relatives to each other. I have stepped out of my comfort zone repeatedly into communities of lighthouse historians, genealogists, and archivists.

At one point, a friend asked to join me on a visit I was making to a descendant of a Baker-related person. I had never met this person. I was unsure, actually, whether the afternoon would yield anything helpful to the project, or if it would be just hours of telling her some stories and listening to her share unrelated memories. All were possible, but I would follow any lead.

My friend was perplexed. "How do you do it, exactly?" she asked. "I want to watch." I could understand her confusion. She knows me well. She knows I am an introvert (Baker Island is my favorite place in the world, after all). How could I drive around, approaching total strangers, and ask for favors? It is out of character. Well . . . I summed it up, "My phone calls begin with, 'This is a long story, and you don't know me, but please don't hang up.' Then, my visits begin with a handshake and introduction. But they always end with hugs."

That really is the best way to describe this journey, one of serendipity and connection. In a society of division and fracture, Baker Island represents both our individuality and our commonalities. Many people expressed, in different words, "Baker Island is *my* special place." But no matter how guardedly and hesitantly they listened to my introductions, they all jumped on board the project. "Oh, Baker Island!" It is like a secret handshake.

The people with whom I have connected over the last year—indeed, the last few decades on the island itself—have been from all over the world, from many walks of life. Baker has long been a hub for fishermen, locals, tourists, summer people, artists, academics, military families, and naturalists. Obviously, it is not the streets of New York. It is an out-of-world experience, a timeless Brigadoon. But I have found Baker Island to bring out the best, where we shed the petty trappings that divide us and discover the fundamental nugget of kindness and cooperation that connects us all. Perhaps, even for a recluse like me, that is the magic of Baker Island.

I have a secret rock on Baker Island, just the right size and place for sitting. Along the front edge, the center section of the rock is more rounded than the sides, worn by hundreds—maybe thousands—of other sitters. How many secrets does it take to smooth granite?

I hope you enjoy reading this as much as I have enjoyed creating it. Just don't tell anyone.

—Cornelia J. Cesari,
November 2017

One

Settlement

Four Generations of Gilleys

William and Hannah Gilley Jr. settled Baker Island around 1806–1812. The date of permanent settlement is unclear. William, like the Abenaki before him, probably fished seasonally from the island for years before clearing land and building a farmhouse for his family, with help from his brother Francis. The next decade saw the establishment of a family of 14 and a near self-sufficient lifestyle. Though Baker Island was isolated many days of the year, off-island needs were few. They transported grain to a Somesville mill and returned three grades of flour, similarly exchanging logs for lumber. An early inventory of livestock listed six cows, a yoke of oxen, several calves and hogs, and a flock of 50 sheep. A variety of vegetables and over 200 bushels of potatoes provided food for family and livestock, and the sea produced bountifully. A little flax and the wool of 50 sheep supplied clothing for the growing family.

Market cash crops included butter, salted fish, cobblestones, and feathers. An island location was no disadvantage when commerce was by coastal schooner.

Their oldest daughter, Hannah II, and Joseph Stanley moved into a new house in 1821, and for the next few years, Hannah I and II alternated birthing. Then Joseph and Hannah Stanley moved to Steuben, and Hannah's brother Elisha moved into their house, where he and his wife (another Hannah) raised nine children.

About that time, in 1828, a lighthouse brought change to Baker. William Gilley's appointment as keeper provided a house and salary. Joseph Stanley became head of the old homestead, where he raised seven children and lived out his life.

The third generation of Gilleys was crucial to the future of Baker Island's settlement. The 16 cousins in Joseph and Elisha's households yielded three permanent residents and an additional house. The fourth generation produced a fourth Gilley household (in addition to the lightkeeper's). Baker's community peaked around 1860–1880 with five households comprising about 25 residents. However, the decline, and ultimate abandonment, of Baker Island was swift and complete by 1930.

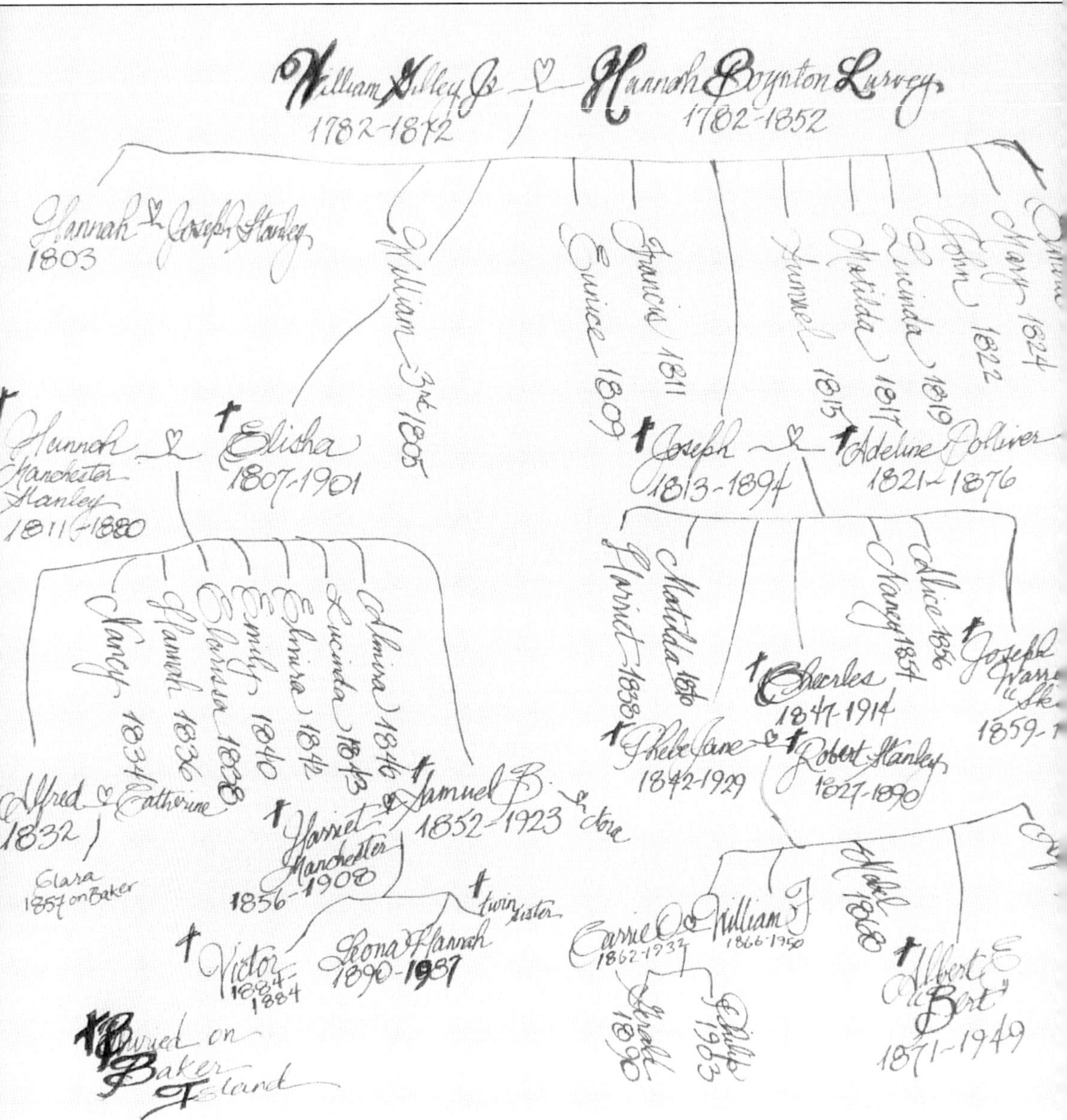

While no known pictures survive of William and Hannah Gilley, descriptions do. William was a large, strong man, over six feet tall and 200 pounds. Hannah, having come from the Lurvey and Boynton families of Massachusetts, was a learned and pious woman. She taught the children, and rowed to church in Southwest Harbor whenever weather allowed. Some of the children and grandchildren were born on Baker Island. Hannah's sister Mary, a midwife married to Joseph Stanley of Fish Point, Great Cranberry, may have come to Baker, or Hannah may have crossed the bar as "her time" neared, or gone to her family in Southwest Harbor. "The Gilley Dozen," children of William and Hannah, bear a resemblance in appearance and character. They settled on nearby islands, in many cases becoming prominent citizens who were widely known and respected. This family tree shows only names and birth dates, unless they remained on Baker Island. Those marked with a cross lie in the Baker Island cemetery. (KOBI.)

By 1812, the Gilleys had built a large farmhouse and barn to accommodate what would become a brood of six sons and six daughters by 1826. Subsequent additions included a connection between house and barn containing a summer kitchen, milk shed, woodshed, outhouse, and the large colonial structure seen below, constructed at a right angle to and enveloping part of the existing house and kitchen. In 1828, a keeper's house would become available to William and Hannah Gilley, and son Joseph would become the head of this household. Here, he and his wife, Adeline Dolliver, raised seven children. Three stayed on the island their whole lives, and others returned regularly. William himself returned to this house around 1859. After Joseph, the house was conveyed to his son Charles, becoming the William/Joseph/Charles Gilley House. (Above, NARA; below, SWHPL No. 12526.)

According to Les Stanley, William Gilley hired workers to hasten construction of this white house northwest of the original farm, decreeing that the living room, kitchen, and one bedroom be finished by New Year's 1821, in time for the January 4 wedding of his oldest daughter, Hannah, to Joseph Stanley. For the next few years, both Hannahs, mother and daughter, were having children in alternating years. After Hannah's first four or five children were born, the family moved to Dyer's Bay, Steuben, around 1834. This farm went to her brother Elisha and then to his son Samuel. It still stands and is owned by Acadia National Park. With their dramatic backdrops of the hills of Mount Desert, these Wyethesque views (above, c. 1916; below, 1937) have been depicted countless times. (Above, Gail M. Carr; below, photograph by Milton Lord; IHS.)

John Gilley was ironically immortalized in *John Gilley: One of the Forgotten Millions* (1899) by Charles W. Eliot, Harvard College president. Gilley went to sea but sold his schooner to buy a Sutton's Island farm. He was active in town affairs and widely respected. Seventy-four-year-old Gilley drowned in 1896 off Bear Island. Mary Ann Carroll, teaching on Baker at the time, bemoaned the weather, "so catching at this season," which prevented her attending his funeral. Gilley's life was also inspiration for Barbara Cooney's *Island Boy*. It is said Matilda Gilley, below, was the only one of William and Hannah Gilley's four youngest daughters to find a husband—accomplished when his ship ran aground on Baker. True or not, Matilda married Oliver Allen and moved to Biddeford. Two Allen granddaughters, Annie and Eunice, visited Baker Island (see page 22). (Right, ANP; below, SWHPL No. 11757.)

Samuel Gilley (below) may be the best documented of the Gilley dozen. He built the Gilley Farm facing Baker Island on Gilley Beach, Islesford, and fished in those waters as well. He married Emily Stanley, and several of their six children figure prominently in the history of both Islesford and Baker. The similarities between "Uncle Sam" in his farm, lifestyle, and personality warrant attention and photographs in this history of his relatives across the bar. The brothers Sam and Elisha (left) were compared by Dr. Vincent Y. Bowditch in August 1896: "We bought milk at old Mr. Elisha Gilley whom I longed to make a snap-shot of; a curious angular old man, rather blind and deaf, brother of our good Mr. Sam Gilley & evidently equally frank!" (Both, ANP.)

Elisha Gilley was born in 1807 on Baker Island and lived there 94 years until his death; he was a widower the last 21 years. Elisha has been described colorfully. Mary Ann Carroll wrote in 1896, "Elisha Gilley is quite smart for a man so old. He was 89 last September. He reminds me a little of my grandfather Lurvey in wanting to have the house still. But he does not like to have the rooms hot as Grandfather did." To simplify matters—or complicate them—Elisha's mother, sister, wife, daughter, niece, and sister-in-law were all named Hannah. (Photograph by Frederick Morse; IHS.)

Elisha Gilley and his wife, Hannah Manchester (left), raised nine children on Baker Island; seven daughters with sons on each end. Their oldest, Alfred, who lived with them, was killed at age 44 in a train crash in Ashtabula, Ohio, on his way to visit his sisters in Nebraska. His widow, Catherine, and daughter Clara (born on Baker in 1857) remained on the island for some time. Elisha's youngest, Samuel Bulger, stayed on Baker, and the house became known as the "Sam B. house." When William Gilley divided the island between the two sons who stayed to farm it, the western half, partially pictured below in 1887, was Elisha's. However, his house was on Joseph's half because the dividing road led behind his house instead of in front of it. (Both, ANP.)

Elisha's daughter Almina Gilley (right) moved to Islesford and married Benjamin Franklin (Frank) Stanley. Two of her sisters, Nancy and Lucinda, married Turners and moved to Nebraska. Nancy, below, married George Turner. According to Susie Wardhaugh, "She was considered to be a 'real lady' so even though she lived in a soddy for awhile, George was determined to build her a proper house. With lumber being in short supply, he swam across the Platte River to an island and cut down trees and then swam them back to the river bank. He built her the first proper house in the town." It is a historic building in Freemont, Nebraska. (Right, ANP; below, Susie Wardhaugh.)

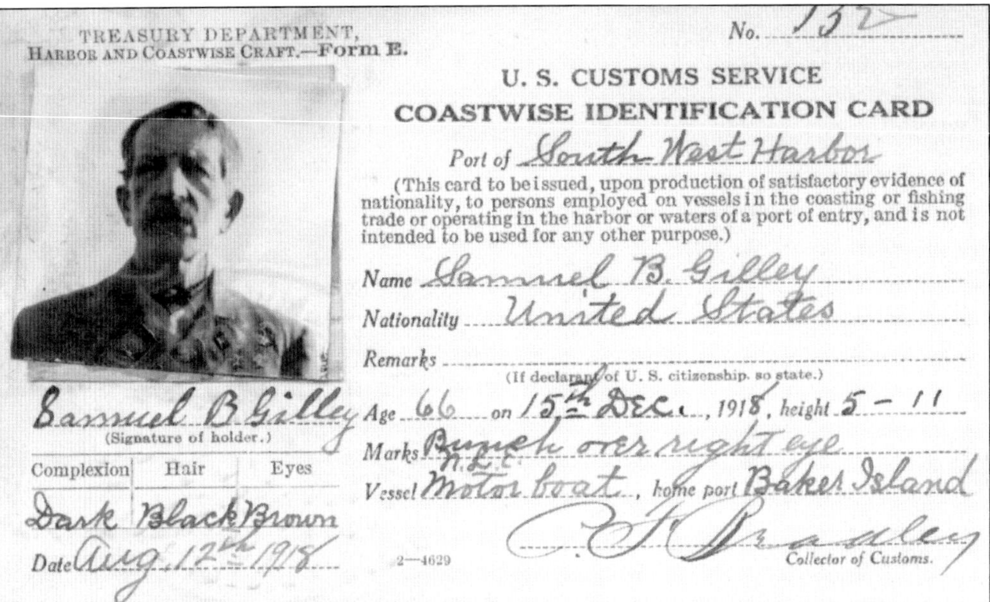
TREASURY DEPARTMENT,
HARBOR AND COASTWISE CRAFT.—Form E.

No. 132

U. S. CUSTOMS SERVICE
COASTWISE IDENTIFICATION CARD

Port of South West Harbor

(This card to be issued, upon production of satisfactory evidence of nationality, to persons employed on vessels in the coasting or fishing trade or operating in the harbor or waters of a port of entry, and is not intended to be used for any other purpose.)

Name Samuel B. Gilley

Nationality United States

Remarks

(If declarant of U. S. citizenship, so state.)

Samuel B Gilley
(Signature of holder.)

Age 66 on 15th Dec., 1918, height 5 – 11

Marks Bunch over right eye

Complexion	Hair	Eyes
Dark	Black	Brown

Vessel Motor boat, home port Baker Island

Date Aug. 12th 1918

2—4629

[signature]
Collector of Customs.

Sam B. Gilley is pictured above on his coastwise identification card, issued during wartime for harbor security. Two generations of large Baker families ended with Sam and Harriet's: two of three babies died, then Harriet died when their daughter Leona was 17. Alfred Stanley wrote, "It don't seem as if I can make myself understand that Hat is dead . . . I pity Sam for I know how much he thought of her. Leona will soon get over it but he never will." Eventually, Sam did remarry, to Nora Higgins. Leona Hannah Gilley Sawyer, pictured at left around age 19, was the last Gilley born on Baker Island. She is remembered, universally, with love and admiration. She is described as feisty and opinionated, gentle but firm. She fiercely valued family, holding her children and grandchildren close. (Above, ANP; left, Martha Sawyer.)

Leona Gilley Sawyer's life was marked by tragedy. Her siblings both died at birth. The school closed when she was a child, and her mother, Harriet, died before Leona moved home. Her daughter Harriet was killed when a spark from the stove ignited the toddler's dress. Her husband, Chester, died at 42, leaving her with four sons; her oldest son and his wife drowned. "He put his life jacket on the dog, and they never found him," Kenny Sawyer recalled. Leona cherished family and friends. Granddaughter Martha recalls holidays "all piled in Nana's house . . . three women in the tiny kitchen, always laughing." Leona loved growing up on Baker but never moved back. Above, at the 1965 New York World's fair are, from left to right, Leona, Mary Carroll, Betty Rich, and Ruth Ballard. At right, around 1949, Leona is seen with Jim and Martha. (Above, Jim and Cessie Sawyer; right, Martha Sawyer.)

Joseph and Adeline Gilley raised seven children on the original Gilley homestead. Three stayed on Baker, while others were nearby, moving back at times. The siblings remained close, exchanging frequent letters and occasional visits; their children relied on the network of aunts and uncles. Lasting bonds were also forged with teachers who boarded on Baker, and members of the lightkeepers' families. This generation had grown up around 1830–1870 on an island buzzing with activity and 16 cousins between Joseph and Elisha's households alone. Pictured above are four of the siblings back at the old homestead. From left to right are Alice, Joseph Warren (known as Warren or "Skipper"), Harriet, and Phebe Jane around 1910. Below are Phebe (nicknamed by the family "Aunt Phe-bob"), Alice, and an unidentified relative. That enormous barn, difficult to maintain, was required for loose storage of winter hay. (Above, SWHPL No. 9375; below, SWHPL No. 9374.)

Charles A. Gilley lived in the family homestead, and his brother Skipper officially lived there when not out at sea. Les Stanley recalls his uncle Skip living in "more or less of a shack, as I remember it—halfway up from the shore up to that ledge, on your left;" however, no structure remains there. The bachelor brothers are buried side by side in the Baker Island cemetery. (ANP.)

William O. Sawtelle, summer resident and historian, described Charles Gilley colorfully around 1920: "Charles Gilley was a character. I knew him well and no picnic to Baker's was complete without a chat with him. Possessed of a keen sense of humor, a fund of anecdote and a refreshing philosophy of life, it is to be regretted that many of his yarns were of too personal a nature to repeat in print." (ANP.)

Gilley family members are pictured outside Charles Gilley's, or the old homestead. From left to right are (sitting) Joseph "Skip" Gilley, Annie and Eunice Allen (unknown which is which), and an unidentified young man; (standing) Harriet "Hat" Gilley Coulter Taylor, Alice Gilley, William Frederick Stanley, Carrie Ober Stanley, and Charles Gilley. The date was around 1917, and the Allen granddaughters (of Matilda Gilley Allen, see page 13) were visiting Baker Island from Biddeford. (SWHPL No. 12010.)

Nancy Gilley (1854–1932), daughter of Joseph and Adeline, married William Doane ("Jimmy") Stanley and moved to Great Cranberry Island. Their niece Esther was living with Aunt Nan and Pa Jim, as they were called, when Charles Gilley brought Phebe Jane over in his boat for a visit of all three siblings. It was rare enough to see Phebe Jane off the island, apparently, that it made an impression worth sharing with her nephew Ralph Stanley. (SWHPL No. 10152.)

Harriet "Hat" Gilley, daughter of Joseph and Adeline, married John Coulter in Massachusetts and had two sons, Charles and Winfred. Charles married Flora Stanley from Islesford. They had a daughter, Ethel, and a son, Edgar, who died at three in 1898. In 1899, Flora died. Hat struggled with her new daughter-in-law. In a letter to her sister, Hat described her discomfort: "I had a good time but today have felt like crying all day. I think what changes Ethel is all carried a way with thing. Tho Mrs. Coulter caused me to stay all night but Phebe the bed spreads are all lace ones and nice at that. That is to much for me that isn't one thing we had. She wants every thing so very nice. . . . She keeps a hired girl, pays her four dollars a week." Hat is pictured at right, and at far right below. (Right, SWHPL No. 9377; below, SWHPL No. 10549.)

In 1862, Phebe Jane Gilley, daughter of Joseph and Adeline, married Civil War veteran Robert Stanley, 15 years her senior. Around 1867, they built this house between her uncle Elisha's house and barn. The main house is now perpendicular to the entry shed, with an eastern dormer. It is the red, privately owned Pearson house. In 1890, Robert Stanley drowned on the fishing weir by the bar. Widowed for four decades, Phebe raised four children. Two sons stayed on Baker; later, daughter Mabel returned home with her children. Only son Alfred flew the nest, settling in Tacoma, Washington. Leona said Phebe Jane was an intelligent and well-read woman. Despite the pleas of friends and relatives, she did not leave Baker Island for her last 36 years, "with the beauty of the mountains and the sea always before her and with contentment in her soul," wrote Fanny Eckstrom. The image below is from 1985. (Left, SWHPL No. 10994; below, Elizabeth Kolm.)

William Frederick Stanley and his bride, Caroline Ober, are pictured below flanking her mother, Ellen, at his mother, Phebe Jane Stanley's, house. In the 1951 aerial photograph above, Will and Carrie's house, built around 1888–1889, is visible on the left, the large white house south of the schoolhouse. They raised two sons on Baker, Gerald and Philip. Carrie Stanley collected postcards sent from all over the country. According to Ralph Stanley, her failing health caused a move to Southwest Harbor, where she died in 1932. Will outlived a second wife, Grace Thompson. Will Stanley's house burned down around 1965. Not intentional vandalism, University of Maine students presumably left a spark in the grass that afternoon, which spread to the house by evening. The blaze was seen from Cranberry Island by young Phil Whitney, but help arrived too late. (Above, USCG; below, SWHPL No. 9373.)

Ethel Coulter, Harriet Gilley's granddaughter, lost her brother when she was five and her mother at age six. Her father, Charles, the Socialist mayor of Brockton from 1899 to 1903, invested in 300 acres of waterfront on Martha's Vineyard. Ethel married Francis Wheeler, but before her first baby was born, her father and stepmother both died of the grippe. Ethel died in 1928, leaving three young children. Pictured above are, from left to right, Ethel, Bert Stanley, Charles, and Skip Gilley. The image at left is identified only as "two Gilley or Stanley women." The two photographs on this page, taken around 1910, may illustrate the social changes described by Harriet on page 23; Gilleys returning to visit might be mistaken for rusticators. (Above, SWHPL No. 10982; left, SWHPL No. 9376.)

Bert Stanley was a good friend to many men, but shy with women, and never married despite continuous prodding and arrangements offered by relatives. Bert Stanley stories abound—that he *always* wore his leather boots and that he had little ambition. He pulled six traps in the morning and six after the noon dinner, then pulled the shades and called it a day. He was described as a permanent fixture in the fish houses down by the shore, sitting and whittling. He did not make anything, just whittled. Les Stanley explained that Bert made lobster claw pegs, buttons for traps, and kindling shavings. The boat name *Agnes* M. could indicate she came from Arthur Ham, who married Bert's second cousin Agnes Maude Gilley. Les had bought his uncle Will's motorboat, which he gave to his uncle Bert when the *Agnes* M. sank at its mooring around 1923. (Above, Dale Robbins; below, ANP.)

ENT,
-Form E.

No. 162

U. S. CUSTOMS SERVICE

COASTWISE IDENTIFICATION CARD

Port of So West Harbor

(This card to be issued, upon production of satisfactory evidence of nationality, to persons employed on vessels in the coasting or fishing trade or operating in the harbor or waters of a port of entry, and is not intended to be used for any other purpose.)

Name Albert E Stanley

Nationality American

Remarks

(If declarant of U. S. citizenship, so state.)

Albert E. Stanley
(Signature of holder.)

Age 47 on May 7, 1918, height 5.8

Marks none

Vessel Agnes M., home port So West Harbor Me

Complexion	Hair	Eyes
Med	Brown	Blue

Date Nov 25 1918

2—4620

P. F. Bradley
Dep Collector of Customs.

After his mother, Phebe Jane's, death in 1929, Bert Stanley remained on Baker only the following summer. He visited the keeper daily, coming and leaving in silence. After that, he lived with his sister Mabel on "too crowded" Great Cranberry Island (pictured). He did not sell his mother's house until 1947. When Stanley died in 1949, nephews Chester, Enoch, and Les, with Arthur Bunker, took his casket to Baker and buried him next to Phebe Jane. Chester's son, renowned boatbuilder Ralph W. Stanley, placed a headstone in 2009. Upon brother Bert's death, Alfred Stanley wrote to surviving siblings Mabel and Will: "I do not doubt but what he has been one of the best boys any woman has ever had. The rest of us went away and tried to live our own lives but he stayed and tried to do all he could for Mother." (Left, GCIHS 2013.259.1990; below, GCIHS 2012.205.1719.)

Two

Government Presence

Lighthouse and Light Station Compound

Baker Island's location, the southwestern entrance to Frenchman's Bay, was deemed vital to coastal navigation and was designated as the site of the first lighthouse in the region. Congress appropriations between 1823 and 1825 for its construction totaled $3,800, but difficulties obtaining deed to the island caused delays. The bidding and construction process is detailed in correspondence between Isaac Ilsley, superintendent of Maine lighthouses, and Stephen Pleasonton, fifth auditor and acting commissioner of revenue in Washington. Pleasonton recommended hiring more qualified Winslow Lewis, but to his frustration, Ilsley contracted with low bidder Jairus Thayer despite Ilsley's own concerns: "Monhegan has now the appearance of negligence of the masonry." Ilsley then hired a relative at $2.25 per day to oversee construction. Lewis fitted up the tower. The 26-foot rubblestone tower, like others built during the period, deteriorated, becoming dangerous and unhealthy for the Gilleys. The mortar failed, so the house and tower were leaky and cold. The stairs were coated in ice in winter, the walls were cracked, and the kitchen, which was added to the four-room rubblestone house, separated from it within a few years.

The tower was fitted with an octagonal lantern, wrought iron frame, and copper dome, and housed 10 lamps. Behind them were 15-inch reflectors arranged two rows high. They were fueled with sperm whale oil, then lard oil. Later, lamps burned kerosene.

In 1855, the tower and keeper's house were replaced by a 43-foot stone tower and wood framed one-and-a-half-story house, connected by a "hyphen," or work room. Eventually the compound expanded to seven buildings. Some were standard lighthouse facilities like the brick oil house; others were repurposed depending upon the needs of the station and the keeper's family. The fuel house was storage for fuel and automobiles, although the first known motor vehicle was not brought to the island for another decade.

Although there are no known photographs of it, an 1857 inspection report records: "Old rubble tower 20 ft high south of tower about 40 ft, good state of preservation." It is unclear when, or whether, it was removed; perhaps the stone was repurposed.

In August 1854, Maine lighthouse superintendent (collector of customs) Luther Jewett decried deplorable conditions at several Thayer lighthouses: "Cement and lime have worked out so much that the water pours in in great abundance. Pointing and whitewashing twice a year is poor economy . . . so badly are they built of cobble stones. The 1853 Annual Report concludes: 'The towers are entirely worthless, lanterns worn out, keepers' dwellings are so old and leaky that they are unhealthy,' " he wrote. "I recommend that both be rebuilt and fitted up with Fresnel lens lights of the fourth or fifth order." Jewett's proposal was approved, and a new lighthouse and lightkeeper's quarters were built on Baker's Island in 1855. This time Congress appropriated $5,000; total expenditures by 1857 were $8,761.33. The tower was fitted with a cutting-edge fourth order Fresnel lens. Developed by physicist Augustin-Jean Fresnel, it allowed a single light source to project 20 miles or more. The lantern was an incandescent oil vapor light requiring hand pumping every few hours to maintain pressure for the vaporizer. (NARA.)

The Fresnel lens was mounted on clockwork. Baker's old "Bull's Eye," according to keeper Ken Sawyer, was wound every four hours to keep it rotating. Baker's designated frequency was a full turn every minute and a half, revealing a flash every 45 seconds as a "bull" passed. In 1895, Dr. Vincent Bowditch wrote of "Capt. Robbins' tale of his patient bravery in sitting up the whole of two nights keeping the light revolving with his hands, the heavy machinery having broken & as he could get no aid from the authorities. He was obliged to keep it going very very slowly & evenly so many parts of a revolution to a minute." Sawyer recalled: "We used to see a lot of birds I never seen before, on the ground. They hit the light during the night . . . I guess they must have thought those bulls, they thought it was the sun and flew into it . . . What a mess! And you pick them up, and there wasn't a whole bone in their body . . . we used to get tags, and send them to the University of Maine." (GHMM.)

In 1955, Baker's fixed flashing light (a steady light with a five-second bright flash every 90 seconds) was discontinued as unnecessary to offshore navigation. Mariners, led by former keeper Cliff Robbins, petitioned successfully to have it reactivated. In spring 1957, it was replaced with a plastic lens and automated 300-mm marine light, flashing rather than fixed flashing. Baker's Fresnel lens is on display at Pemaquid Point Lighthouse. In June 2017, the US Coast Guard Aids to Navigation team upgraded the lantern to a solar-powered Vega VLB 44 LED. Since 1957, Baker Island Light 2045 has been listed as a flashing white with 10-second period. The nominal range is 10 nautical miles, 105 feet above sea level, and its coordinates are 44-14-28.351 north, 068-11-56.442 west. (Above, KOBI; left, Nathan Hamilton, USCG.)

In 1903, the brick tower was reinforced with the construction of a second layer of bricks enveloping the first. The windows were then reset in the new outer wall. Post-1903 photographs show a tower with less taper to the lantern deck and less overhang of the iron deck itself. In light tower design, windows were strategically located to maximize natural lighting on the stairs. A 43-foot tower had 43 steps, which the keeper had to climb and descend four times a night. The lightkeeper at Baker Island took 5,332 icy steps up and 5,332 icy steps down in the dark every January. (Both, KOBI.)

The keeper's quarters were built in 1855; these rear views are from the southwest. The main door faces north, with a cellar bulkhead on the east. The cellar, cemented in 1880, held a cistern and a coal-fired steam furnace. These photographs show the north-south ell added onto the southeast corner of the 1855 structure. Although park records report the date as 1875, the 2008 Condition Assessment Report states that the nail type would indicate this occurred prior to 1870. Comparing these pictures from 1897 and 1958, one can see the dormer, added between 1898 and 1905. At some point the entryway and steps were added. Also, note the obstructed view to the water on the eastern side, formerly the Joseph/Charles Gilley farm. (Both, NARA.)

In 1853, the government built a boathouse for the lightkeeper's use on the island's north shore. More than one keeper preferred his own boat to the heavy one provided. The building exemplified boathouses in this region as documented by the National Register of Historic Places; the structure measured 30 feet by 12 feet and had a wood foundation, frame, and siding. There was also a ramp, about 100 feet long, with wooden rails on wooden posts. Boats could be hauled up or launched with the use of a hand-operated winch (a hurdy-gurdy), remains of which are still on the shore. One can also find drilled stones leading to the water, which were footings for the launchway. Visible to the west are remnants of a Gilley fish house. Just to the east was a small fish house for the lightkeeper. (Right, NARA; below, USCG.)

The 30-square-foot privy was 40 feet south-southeast of the lighthouse. Donna Madison recalls visiting her grandfather, keeper Frank Faulkingham, as a six year old. The two-and-a-half holer made quite an impression; the bench dropped down for a child-sized seat. With little children, a winter night trek to the "back house" was surely a family affair! Below, the 1905 paint locker between the keeper's house and the outhouse, along the existing wooden walkway, was for safely storing flammable materials, as was the 1895 oil house. The one-story paint locker measured about 18.5 feet by 16.5 feet and had a stone foundation, wooden shingles on the roof, and exterior walls. This photograph is from about 1958. The area where the paint locker stood grew up quickly after the building collapsed. Recent clearing has revealed a number of artifacts; visitors are trusted to leave them undisturbed. (Both, NARA.)

An 1895 brick oil house held combustible kerosene, which replaced sperm oil and lard oil. North of the tower on a concrete slab, the oil house measures 100 square feet. A wooden walkway on granite piers crossed the uneven terrain to the light tower. Each morning by 10:00 a.m., the keeper filled the tank in the tower. After 1937, concrete and brick cradles for two metal drums were added east of the structure (see page 46). The cradles and walkway piers remain. The 1905 fuel house (garage or barn), 200 feet west of the tower, measures about 19.5 feet by 13 feet. The structure has a wood post foundation and loft above the ground floor. Whatever its previous purposes, it now provides valuable tool and equipment storage for Acadia and KOBI island and building maintenance. (Both, NARA.)

This comprehensive 1952 aerial view shows almost all of the structures that comprised the Baker Island Light Station compound. Even all 150 linear feet of wooden walkways are intact. At upper left, 300 feet north of the tower, is the foundation of the first keeper's house (1828). The deep rectangle to the left was probably the main house, with the kitchen to the right and a porch extending back on the eastern corner. Also gone is the white "U.S. Barn," which stood in about the same spot. The lightkeeper would have kept his livestock there until the 1905 garage/barn was built (lower left), which has room for a few animals and hay storage overhead. This rare image shows the second structure beside it. Based on log book entries, this might have served as a hen house. (USCG.)

Three

Shipwrecks and War

Coast Guard, Lifesaving Service, and Signal Corps

The area around Baker Island has been called a "ship trap." The lightkeeper could not leave his post in a storm, so in 1878, a United States Life-Saving Service station was established on the Islesford point across the bar. The courageous surfmen saved crews and sometimes cargo.

Among the numerous shipwrecks were the *St. Leon* in 1854; *Savinia Clark*, 1856; *Aerolite*, 1869; *Shamrock*, 1882; *Water Lily*, 1886; *Afton*, 1887; *Byrtle*, 1892; *Abbott*, 1896; *Three Sisters*, 1908; and *Seth Nyman*, 1921. A mysterious unmanned 95-foot schooner, the *Lucerne*, of New Brunswick, was discovered on December 1, 1893.

Not all wrecks were unintentional, however. "Those rocks were a great place for ship companies to wreck their ships on purpose for the insurance. That used to be a great game," Alfred Stanley recalled. "I remember when I was a kid one ship laid off shore in the nice weather for days, and as soon as it got foggy they ran it ashore. The captain got us kids to pile the stuff on the beach, and peel off the copper sheathing from the hull." Ships' crews and some island residents were cut in. Alfred recalled sleeping on sheets from a stolen bolt of silk, hidden under William Gilley's sleeping wife, Hannah. "Nobody respected English property," he said. "Old time Yankees up there still hate the British, just the way the rebels down South still can't forgive us Yankees."

During World War II, German submarines frequented the Maine coast. Fishermen described encounters with surfacing U-boats. Francis Fernald reacted by firing his shotgun at one until the enemy submerged. Tommy Spurling, stunned by a polite request for lobsters—in flawless English—complied. Keeper Frank Faulkingham claimed that "a dozen armed Germans" pilfered fuel in the night from light station drums while he retreated safely into the house. Calvin Alley reported that two draggers were sunk, sending the 40 combined crew to the US Life-Saving Service station, where he was on duty. A rumor, later confirmed by Civil Defense warden Mae Salisbury, told of U-boats brazenly passing through Western Way and up Somes Sound to Man-o-War Brook—so named because a sheer drop-off provided deepwater access to ships charging their freshwater tanks.

There were hundreds of Coast Guard personnel in the area between Baker's Coastal Lookout Station, Islesford's station, and Southwest Harbor's lighthouse/buoy depot, which became the centralized US Coast Guard Station SWH around 1945.

The Guardsmen sometimes picked up mail for Baker folks, who would cross the bar to retrieve it. Lightkeepers would walk or boat across and ride to Southwest Harbor in the launch for supplies. The 1905 crew above are, from left to right, George Gilley, Fred Phippen, John Bunker holding Togo the cat, Smith Stanley, Arthur Fernald, and Willie Spurling (rear). "You *have* to go out," the command went. "You don't have to come back, but you have to go out." Below, John D. Phippen, Walter Hadlock, and Milton Phippen are shown bringing the mail during the big freeze of 1923. During the winter of 1922–1923, the harbor completely froze over. This was not unique; it had happened in 1919. Making the best of it, folks from the Cranberry Isles hiked across the ice for provisions, hauling sleds or their watercraft lashed to runners. (Both, IHS.)

The connection between the lighthouse and the station was not just the one-mile bar or telephone line—especially after 1930, when they were sole neighbors. Ken Sawyer served at the US Life-Saving Service station and also on Baker Island. "They had a radio on the station, not the lighthouse. Must have stood high as the ceiling . . . we listened to music, and when they had Jack Dempsey, an old prizefight, never missed one of them! And all those fellas . . . the baseball service, they all went crazy over that." The crew patrolled the beach and practiced using equipment. Shown here in 1887 are drills with a lifeboat (above) and a Lyle gun. The canon fired a line nearly 700 yards to rig a ship-to-shore conveyance system. Survivors were then reeled in strapped into a breeches buoy. (Both, ANP.)

One frigid January night in 1923, two schooners wrecked in the Cranberry Isles. The *Don Parsons* (above) and the *General George B. Hogg*, from Nova Scotia, were carrying coal from New York. The *Bar Harbor Times* lauded: "In both cases the crews were rescued by Captain W.I. Brown and the members of his United States Coast Guard crew at Islesford. The work of the Coast Guard men is described by the rescued mariners and by seafaring men of this section as being remarkably fine work reflecting great credit upon Captain Brown, his men and the service that they represent." The 1,000 tons of coal spilled (below) and trapped in the hold proved too tempting, and many residents recall retrieving two winters' worth of fuel. The insurance company charged the looters $6 per ton. (Both, ANP.)

In December 1896, the *Bar Harbor Record* reported: "Schooner *Abbott* of Parsboro, NS, wrecked on Bakers Island. She had on board 160 tons of grindstones, and no doubt grindstones will be plentiful around these shores next year." Indeed, at least one is still on Baker, and one was sunk as a mooring. Teacher Mary Carroll wrote, "The Whitmore boys came to take out the grindstones. They got six of the largest out of the hold and left them on deck. They were about seven feet by fourteen inches." It is said that Jack, the shipwrecked dog at right, refused to return to Canada and became a mascot for Islesford instead of the *Don Parsons*. (Both, ANP.)

The US Life-Saving Service station (above, 1939) became a US Coast Guard station in 1915. After the war, all Coast Guard operations in the region were centralized in Southwest Harbor, and this station became a private residence. In February 1943, Lyle Stepanek was stationed on Islesford and then transferred to the Baker Island Coastal Lookout Station, shown below in 1952. Stepanek wrote to his mother in Iowa, "I am on coast patrol. Walk the beach for four hours at a stretch and lay off eight hours. I also stand watch in a tower. Got to make weather reports and handle the telephone switchboard . . . boy what walks. It's snowing blowing hard (quite a storm)." He warned, "Mother, this war is getting closer. Can't tell you much about it. But it's very close now to U.S. I ain't kidding." (Above, NARA; below, USCG.)

During the Spanish-American War, utility poles carried telegraph lines across Baker Island to the shore, then to Northeast Harbor via Islesford and Bear Island, financed with national defense appropriation. A US Signal Service building was established south of the lighthouse, along with a flagstaff (see page 53). The rare image below demonstrates use of the signal cross for communication, possibly with those manning the cannon placed at the entrance to Frenchman's Bay. Dr. Vincent Bowditch lamented in August 1898: "Telegraph poles traverse the little island now connected with the only sign of war here—the big signal station at Baker's on which we can see the great signal cross looming up near the light house." A 1942 lookout tower was built on the same location for submarine spotting and also signaling. Logbooks regularly noted "wig-wag and semaphore practice." (Above, NARA; below, USCG.)

Concrete fuel tank cradles were installed around 1937. Frank Faulkingham had been on Baker since 1932; during the war, he had five young men under his charge. Lyle Stepanek wrote, "I got on a swell place now. Don't walk the beach any more, just stand watches in this tower and keep the lighthouse burning. This place is just like home. They have a cow, a calf, dog and a pup (did have six but sold five) and he did have some chickens when I first came here but we put the finishings to them. I got the job of milking right away and taking care of the cow and calf. This island is only a half mi long and is mostly rock. This house is built right on top of a rock." (Above, MDIHS; left, Nancy Stepanek Rosburg.)

Lyle Stepanek continued, "I was in the Tower and got a phone call . . . Saying to stop a Navy Cutter going by the Island and send it back to Bar Harbor, it's very important. . . . I had to use a spotlight and send the Morse Code. Finally they turned around and went back. . . . That's part of our job. . . . I get what we call it (Island Happy) or in other words nutty. That's just an expression we use for the fun of it. We boys have lots of fun here." Stepanek duck-hunted, went fishing, and drove a boat. "I really got to like this place," he wrote. "Some say it's the best on the East Coast—if you'd ask me I'd say it was." Stepanek, who was engaged, went to sea in September and was lost in March 1944. (Both, Nancy Stepanek Rosburg.)

On July 2, 1944, fishermen Ernest and Merrill Stanley reported observing a periscope and submarine hull about 13 miles off Baker Island. A K-14 blimp was deployed from Massachusetts. Although lightly armed, blimps normally reported observations to a destroyer escort, but this one was alone. Around 10:00 p.m., the blimp went down. The official account was "crash due to pilot error," but witness accounts, wreckage, and survivors disagree. Evidence suggests a firefight took place; two depth charges had been dropped and the .50-caliber machine gun fired. The blimp was peppered with holes consistent with German antiaircraft fire. Six Navy crewmen were lost; four survivors were whisked away and ordered silent. The wreckage was towed to Bunker's Cove in Islesford and guarded. Might U-boat wreckage lie off Baker's coast? (Both, US Navy photographs; Earl Brechlin.)

Four

Ownership

Competing Claims and Ulterior Motives

When William Gilley was removed as lighthouse keeper in 1849, he moved out to farm Great Duck Island. Joseph and Elisha Gilley did not welcome the new lightkeeper, John Rich, who complained in March 1852 that the Gilleys "abuse and insult me at every opportunity." Government officials corresponded for years about legal options, warrants, writs, and penalties; they sent a treasury cutter to serve notice. After the revenue cutter *Alert* served the Gilleys in 1852, Captain Whitcomb reported that "they talked very fair to me on the subject and wanted to have the thing settled." Whether by lighthouse board savvy, by the Gilleys' design, or by coincidence, keeper John Rich was replaced by three successive cousins of the Gilleys. William Gilley's first cousin Joseph Bunker was in effect the government representative while a peaceful—and favorable— agreement was offered to the Gilleys. Bunker's father, Joseph Sr., was the brother of Gilley's mother, Eunice; both were grandchildren of Benjamin Bunker, first settler of Great Cranberry Island.

Fifty years had passed since Gilley's 1806 settlement, so his claim of undisputed ownership was deemed too difficult to refute. The generous 1855 agreement stipulated that the government would maintain a reservation of about 19 acres—10 containing the light station, nine for a fog signal, and a right-of-way to the landing and boathouse, as well as pasturage rights for the keeper. The Gilleys retained the remainder of the island.

The issue was resurrected in 1898; again, the Town of Cranberry Isles had a financial interest. The town had voted to buy a plot of land and erect a schoolhouse on Baker Island and had done so, but Sam B. Gilley had no deed to the plot. In an 1898 letter from the US attorney in Portland to the attorney general, he addressed the issue, concluding that it would be "unfair and oppressive at this late day to assert the paramount title of the Government as against the few poor and hardy fishermen living there . . . I can see no earthly objection to allowing the town of Cranberry Isles to build a schoolhouse for the proper education of their youth."

A different legal outcome could have had far-reaching ramifications affecting wealthy American families and international economics based on groundwork laid in the 17th century.

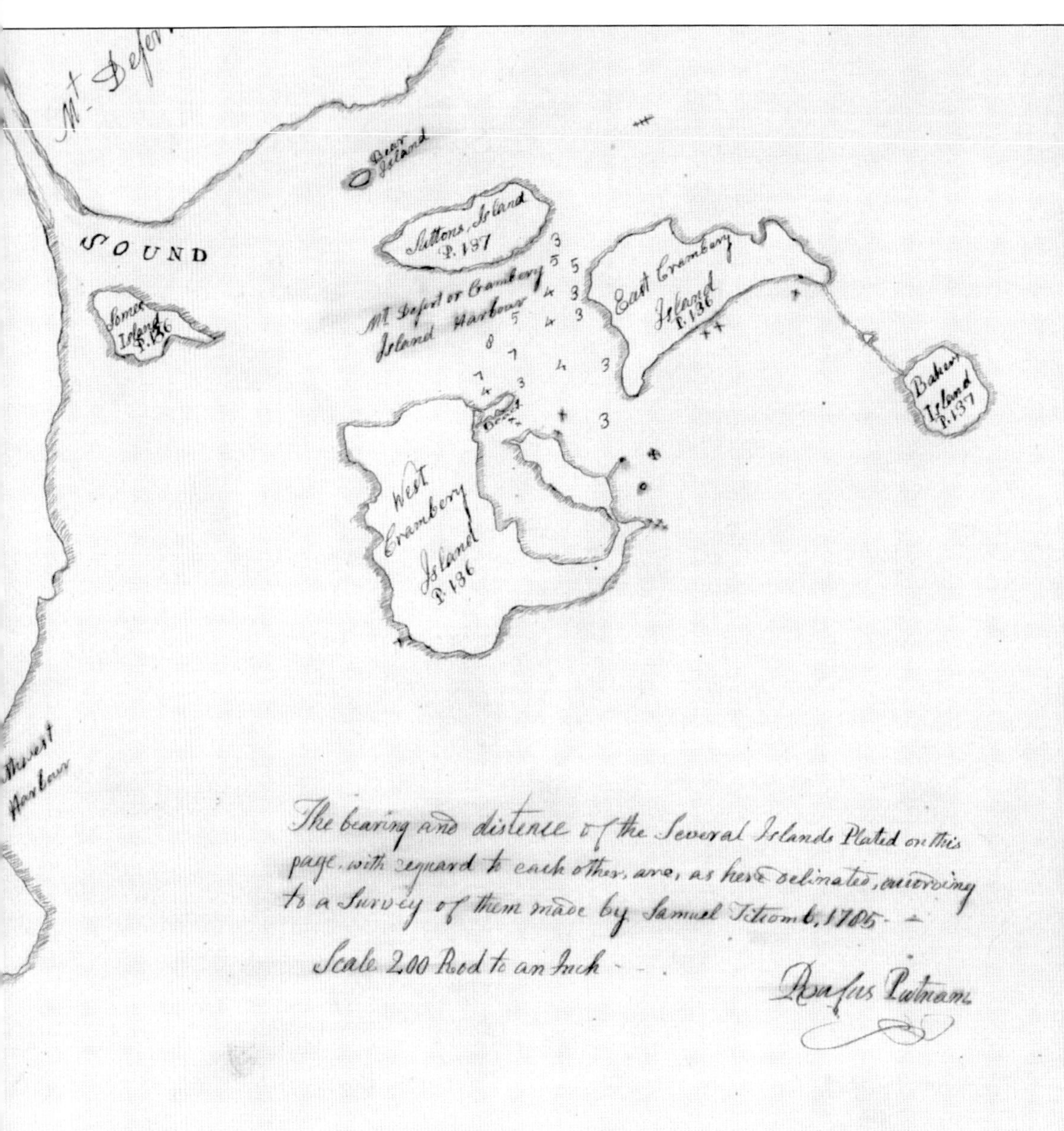

In 1785, this survey was drawn up in preparation for sale of tracts of Massachusetts's "Eastern Lands" to pay off war debt. Barthelemy and Maria Theresa De Gregoire then arrived from France to lay claim; King Louis had granted lands, including Baker Island, to Maria's grandfather, Cadillac, in 1688. A grateful Francophile nation naturalized her family and granted her 60,000 acres. After selling most of the grant in 1792 to Henry Jackson of Boston, the couple lived modestly in Hulls Cove. Jackson, in 1796, sold his claim to William Bingham, who died in 1803. Bingham, of Philadelphia, was perhaps the richest man in America, with international banking connections. He was deeply involved with the powerful Baring brothers of London banking; not only were they in business, but Henry and Alexander Baring each married one of Bingham's daughters. Bingham, by his death, had purchased over two million acres in Maine. Other titles had been contested in Massachusetts General Court and held up. His heirs then sold Baker's Island to the US government for $300 in 1827. (Maine State Archives.)

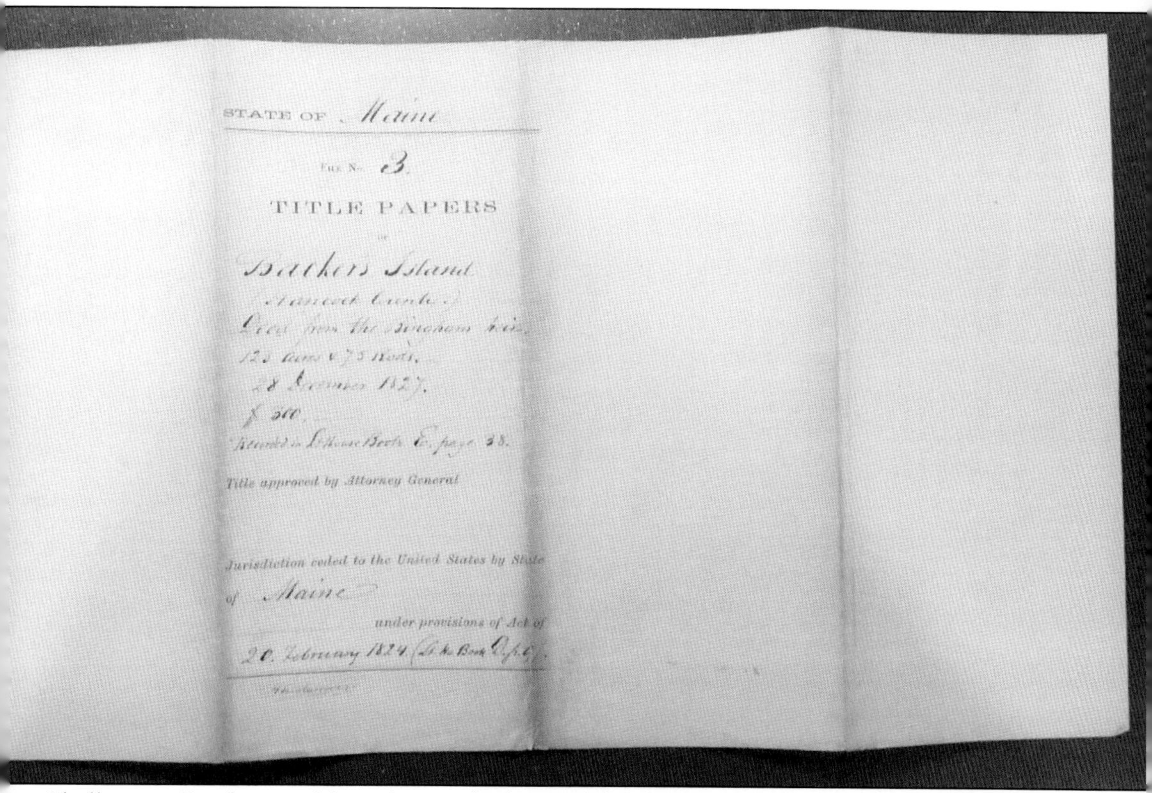

Challenging Bingham in Massachusetts had caused the demise of the Federalists, establishing the bipartisan Republican/Democrat system still in effect today. Maine was no longer part of the commonwealth, and it was time for new precedent. The potential ramifications for area landowners—now some of the most influential Americans in society—were tremendous. Bingham's heirs were powerful British bankers; if the government won its case, validating this deed, land all over coastal Maine could be lost to the Barings and their noble relations. Estates wrested from England and then Massachusetts could revert to British ownership. Les Stanley recalled that summer people liked to draw water from Gram's well and visit with her. "I guess they liked her, so they hired a fancy Portland lawyer." Whether summer people hired Benjamin Thompson or not, he represented the 13 landowners on Baker Island as well as the Town of Cranberry Isles and won. He billed the town only $100. A 1909 US Circuit Court ruling finally settled the matter. The town would receive taxes, property deeds were secure, and Gilleys began transferring land. (NARA.)

Another interested party was William P. Preble (left), chairman of the Selectboard of the Town of Cranberry Isles. He may have appeared to side with the Gilleys, but he was an energetic advocate for the town's coffers. Preble wrote to Washington, DC, "If the United States can't manage their affairs . . . from the appearances it would seem that Mr. Gilley was the owner of the Island. What we would like to know respecting the business is who is the owner of Baker Island and if it belongs to Mr. Gilley we can see no good reason why he should not be taxed for it." Below, in a photograph taken sometime between 1880 and 1895, the fence marking the 10-acre government reservation is visible. (Left, GCIHS 1000.0.1066; below, NARA.)

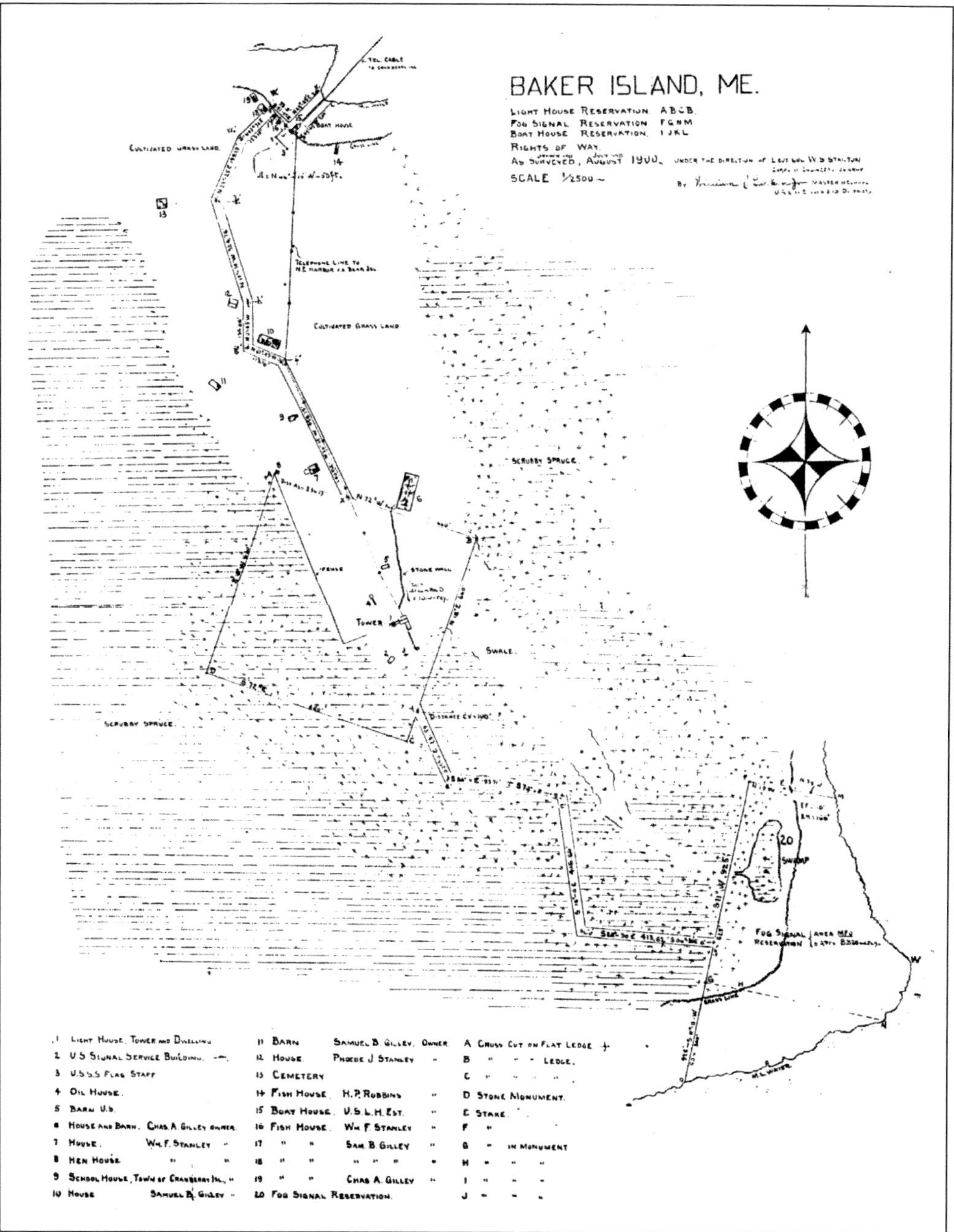

This 1900 survey lays out the 1898 ruling by the US attorney in Portland. The rights-of-way are marked, as are the reservations: 10 acres for the light station, nine for the fog signal on the south shore; and a boathouse reservation. It was determined that the government owned only the land on which the tower sits and waived title to anything not included in the 1855 agreement. Structures added after this survey include a government paint locker southeast of the keeper's house (c. 1900), a fuel house/garage/barn west of the keeper's house (1905), and a 30-foot watchtower near the structure labeled "2" (c. 1942). Pictures are also dated effectively by the placement of a 40-foot steel flagpole (1937) and two oil tanks on concrete cradles (sometime after 1937). (NARA.)

Baker was divided between Joseph and Elisha Gilley, bisected by Main Street. To confuse matters, Elisha's farm was on the eastern side (Joseph's), and Joseph's daughter and grandson (Phebe and Will Stanley) had houses on the western side (Elisha's). In 1909, legal deeds became available, but 20 years later, Baker was deserted. Residents had died, and scattered heirs had differing relationships with Baker. In the 1920s, Ethan and Florence Underwood from New Jersey bought Sam B.'s house and the western half from Leona and Nora, and Will's house from him. Some of Joseph's heirs (Joseph and Winfred E. Coulter, sons of Harriet's son Winfred M. Coulter) attempted to consolidate holdings of the eastern half, collecting inherited fractions and buying rights from cousins in the 1920s. In 1976, they sued to affirm those rights, then donated their half to the National Park Foundation. The Underwoods had donated their property to the Nature Conservancy. Ultimately, the vast majority ended up as national park land, except three lots in non-Gilley private hands. The heirs and descendants were left with only the cemetery. (NARA.)

Joseph Coulter (1887–1977) is shown at right around 1912. In 1949, Alfred Stanley wrote: "Win's boys are young and could have a good time there. I bet that old cellar up at the old house is still as good as it used to be and with a little fixing would be good to build on. I can't understand why young Win waited so long to act on this thing. . . . I wished the Coulters had started things before most of us were dead or almost so." In 1976, the Coulters transferred ownership to the National Park Foundation. According to Les Stanley, Win said that the park would "take it away eventually" and he felt pressured to donate the land. Winfred E. Coulter's (1905–2001) headstone is on Baker. He died in Florida just months after his wife, Edna. (Right, Mildred Chalmers; below, NARA.)

Acadia National Park has gradually acquired the vast majority of Baker Island. The only exceptions are the cemetery, the two red buildings, and the Dance Floor. Above in 2012, longtime interpretive ranger Kirk Lurvey addresses one of hundreds of groups to whom he has introduced Baker Island. A local schoolteacher, Lurvey has maintained his commitment to this seasonal job at least one day a week for decades. His personal dedication to Baker Island runs in his blood; as a Lurvey, he is related to Hannah Lurvey Gilley. Below, another relative, the late schoolhouse owner Elizabeth Kolm, works on her roof. Note the period-correct homemade flag. As a Bunker, she was related to William Gilley. The two private residences are well cared for; both have recent new roofs and extensive foundation work. (Above, KOBI; below, Kolm family.)

Five

Lighthouse Keepers

From "Other" Residents to Only Residents

The Baker Island Lighthouse was manned by at least 18 keepers before its 1957 automation. Eleven shared the island with the Gilleys. Their terms ranged from one to 21 years; their households from one to about nine—both saving the school and closing it. Babies were born, children and wives died. Keepers and their families befriended and married Gilleys, teachers, and Coast Guardsmen. The inhabitants of the house on the hill had a tremendous impact on the Baker Island community.

Lightkeeping duties evolved. Pumps, machinery, and motor vehicles lightened labor while wages increased, from $350 in 1828 to $1,680 in 1928, when Vurney King summarized his responsibilities: "I have 7.5 tons of coal, 400 gal of oil, annual provisions, wood, lumber for repairs to be hauled ¼ mile from shore. Seven structures and fence to maintain, two acres to mow. Lighthouse duties: Care and operation of a 4th order incandescent oil vapor light and lens revolving clock. Routing work commencing at sunset: light the light, pump up pressure of air, wind clock that revolves the lens; 9pm: wind clock, pump up pressure; midnight: wind clock, pump air; sunrise: put out light, wipe off lens, clean brass, put cover on lens, fill tank with oil, pump up pressure, dust down through tower, clean vaporizer, wash, paint when needed. Three miles by water to Post Office and Stores I have to go get my own mail and provisions." When there was no island school, children boarded elsewhere or mother and children stayed off-island except summers.

In 1896, Dr. Vincent Bowditch recounted this exchange: " 'Captain Robbins, think what we owe to you for your faithful service here so many years!' His face grew very serious as he said 'I have been a sea captain & I know what a lighthouse means to one at sea!' Whenever I look from my window and see the bright flash across the water towards me, I think of the faithful watcher & feel grateful to him. How much we take for granted & how little we realize what such faithfulness means."

Stephen Pleasonton recommended Samuel Moody as the first lightkeeper. His letter was marked: "Let William Gilly [sic] be appointed. J.Q. Adams." Why the president himself interfered is unknown. William and Hannah Gilley moved into the keeper's house and kept the light for over 20 years, earning $350 annually. When the Whigs were elected, according to Charles Eliot, Gilley said, "with some expletives, that he would not change his political connection for all the lighthouses in the United States" and was replaced by John Rich. Gilley's sons, Elisha and Joseph, allegedly harassed Rich mercilessly. Superintendent Jewett praised Rich's perseverance: "If Mr. Rich, present keeper of the Light-House would vacate the place he would put a man there that would leave the Island very quick." Rich's replacement, however, was the boys' cousin Joseph Bunker (first cousin to their father, William Gilley). Whether Rich was driven out for Bunker's sake, or Bunker was hired to make peace, harmony ensued. An agreement was reached in 1855. Bunker was followed by his brother Rev. John Elisha Bunker (1856–1860, cover photograph) and then their nephew Warren Bunker. Elisha's daughter married another nephew, William Bunker. This photograph was taken around 1879. (SHPL.)

Alden Jordan served from 1867 to 1883, following Freeman Young (1861–1867). Jordan's 10-year-old son Freddie was born and died on Baker. Then cancer struck his wife, Mercy. In 1883, a *Bar Harbor Times* correspondent wrote: "I met the lightkeeper, Mr. Jordan, looking well in health after this long, cold winter, but feeling very sad indeed at the loss of his wife. I missed her kind face very much." Dora, their daughter, "had all the charge of the house and the care of her late estimable mother during the latter's long and exhausting sickness, never wavered in her filial duty." Alden Jordan Jr. married Margaret Gilley, Sam's daughter (see Sam, page 14). Jordan then spent 16 years at Bear Island Light, where he witnessed John Gilley's (page 13) dory capsize in a gale. He repeatedly blew his horn, bringing help, but it was too late. (Right, NEHPL; below, NARA.)

Roscoe G. Lopaus (1845–1912) served as lightkeeper from 1883 to 1888 with his wife, Anna Rebecca Kelley (1844–1920). Pictured in front of them are daughters Mollie, left, and Annie. The boys are likely two of their three sons, Roy, Andrew, and Roscoe. Nineteenth-century lightkeeping was arduous, but Lopaus had served in the Maine 1st Heavy Artillery Regiment, which suffered one of the highest casualty rates in the Civil War. He survived trench warfare during the Siege of Petersburg. (SWHPL No. 11701.)

This is an unusual view of the lighthouse from the south. The 1905 paint locker is not yet built between the outhouse and keeper's house, nor is the 1905 fuel house (which stands to the left) as evidenced by the lack of stairs down to it. It is pre-dormer (1898–1905), and the second layer of brick (1903) is not on the tower. (NARA.)

Howard P. Robbins served from 1888 to 1902. In the photograph above, Robbins walks between two fish houses to the shore to meet the revenue cutter *Woodbury*, visible approaching from the north. Below, he is likely pictured with his son Clifford. Eliza Robbins moved to Southwest Harbor with most of the children for school, while Clifford stayed on Baker. Howard Robbins's brother Samuel also lived on Baker for a time, but the men had to "keep their own house" until New Year's Eve 1899. That stormy winter night, Clifford married Pansy Lovering in Southwest Harbor and rowed her back to Baker Island. Clifford was an unpaid, unofficial assistant keeper until the father and son became the first keeper and assistant at the new Rockland Breakwater Light in 1902. In 1955, Clifford Robbins led the successful protest to reactivate the Baker Island light (see page 78). (Above, ANP; below, SWHPL No. 5050.)

George S. Connors's 13-year service, from 1902 to 1915, was especially eventful on a personal level. On March 13, 1904, his wife, Addie, died after a few days' painful illness, leaving behind their week-old infant daughter. Leah Connors was raised until age seven by her grandmother in Lubec. Below, a rare photograph shows the white government barn north of the lighthouse. This may have been the keeper's barn attached to the first rubblestone house. When the fuel house/garage was built to the southwest in 1905, perhaps lumber from this barn was used for that or the second structure next to it. Dated between 1895 and 1898, this photograph is post–oil house, pre-dormer, and pre-telegraph. (Left, LHD, Carol Moffatt; below, USCG.)

TREASURY DEPARTMENT,
HARBOR AND COASTWISE CRAFT.—Form E.

No. [illegible]

U. S. CUSTOMS SERVICE
COASTWISE IDENTIFICATION CARD

Port of So. West Harbor

(This card to be issued, upon production of satisfactory evidence of nationality, to persons employed on vessels in the coasting or fishing trade or operating in the harbor or waters of a port of entry, and is not intended to be used for any other purpose.)

Name George S. Connors

Nationality American

Remarks

(If declarant of U. S. citizenship, so state.)

George S Connors
(Signature of holder.)

Age [illegible] on Jan 13, 1918, height 5.8

Marks None

Vessel Leah, home port So. West Harbor

Complexion	Hair	Eyes
Med.	Gray	Blue

Date Dec 4, 1918

2—4629

F. F. Bradley
[illegible]
Collector of Customs.

Coastwise identification cards were issued for maritime security. George Connors's boat was named *Leah*. Although without a family, Connors was not without "man's best friend." A humorous account from two years after he was widowed was written by Dr. Vincent Bowditch: "We went to Baker's and walked down to the superb rocks and watched the surf for some time, then returned to the top of the island and before sunset ate our supper accompanied by 'Max' the light-house doggie who after some disturbance seemed to finally recognize us and gave the stamp of his approval. After making overtures against a convenient tree he silenced his voice and approached us wagging his tail. Very fat since he greeted us here two years ago. I fear the swill-tub has been attacked much too often for beauty of contour." (Above, ANP; right, Mildred Chalmers.)

In August 1906, Dr. Vincent Bowditch wrote of a trip to Baker: "Beautiful sunset. Friendly greetings & assistance from Mr. Connors the keeper, & his housekeeper Mrs. Steele, of long gray ringlets & 'store teeth' which made her smile 'a mineral benediction' as Holmes says." A later advertisement for a housekeeper yielded one, Mary Cole Moore (1864–1942, pictured), who became his bride in March 1910. (Mildred Chalmers.)

In 1910, Bowditch "saw the new Mrs. Connors at the lighthouse and got her to boil coffee and give us butter. She naively said when I asked her how much it would all be 'Oh, I leave that to you' and as I said 'Will a dollar be all right?' she replied 'Oh yes! I usually find I do better when I leave it to others to name the price!' " (Mildred Chalmers.)

The widowed Mary Cole Moore Connors had four children by Charles Moore (1856–1900): Edwin (b. 1882), Galen (b. 1883), Russell (b. 1889), and daughter Gussie (b. 1897). The boys were in their 20s, and Gussie was 13 when Mary married keeper Connors. George Connors's daughter Leah, now seven, moved in with her father. These pictures show the boys when their father was still living: Edwin and Galen at right and Russell below. Russell later served at the lifesaving station across the bar in Islesford and married Baker Island schoolteacher Gertrude Demmons (page 87). (Both, Mildred Chalmers.)

This blended family began a second population surge on Baker Island, prompting a brief reopening of the schoolhouse and connections between residents, visitors, lighthouse keepers, and teachers. The contrast between the first and second halves of Connors's tenure demonstrates the impact of a lightkeeper's family (or lack thereof) on the Baker community. Pictured above on the keeper's house steps sometime between 1910 and 1913 are, from left to right, (first row) Gussie Moore; (second row) George S. Connors, Leah, and Mary Cole Moore Connors. (Above, Mildred Chalmers; below, MDIHS.)

Les Stanley recalled of Leah (right; also pages 84 and 85): "I didn't go on Baker's again, [until] I was 21 or 22. And that's the first time I was up in the lighthouse. My brother Chester would be in the lighthouse half of the time. As a kid, I was bashful. Connors had a girl there about my age, and I kept away from the girls when I was 10 years old." Gussie Moore (below) shared Baker stories with her daughter-in-law Mildred. While working at her aunt's Vinalhaven boardinghouse, Moore met Scottish stonecutter Frank Chalmers. They courted through the mail. Moore would call postmistress Alva Beal. If she had mail, she would run across the bar and back on the tide. If prevented by weather or tide, Beal would open the letter and read it to her. (Both, Mildred Chalmers.)

Pictured is a gathering at the lighthouse around 1914. George and Mary Connors were happy together and had joyous times on Baker Island with friends and extended family. Sadly, George's health declined, and he resigned his position as lightkeeper in 1915. The family moved to Manset and remained a part of that community thereafter. Mary was to be widowed a second time, with George's death in 1919, and married her third husband, John Judkins, in 1927. Gussie Moore died too young as well, at age 50; Leah Connors married and had a daughter of her own. The family ties that formed on Baker Island endured. One of Moore's grandchildren traveled from Virginia to attend a 2016 graveside ceremony honoring her step-great-grandfather George Connors's service as a lighthouse keeper, fearing there would be no one left to represent him. (Mildred Chalmers.)

Vurney King, son of sea captain Merrill King, came to Baker Island from Saddleback Light, followed two weeks later by his family, wife Maude Lizzie Kaler King (1875–1976); sons Reginald (b. 1894), Merrill (b. 1897), and Pearl (b. 1900); and daughters Edna (b. 1906) and Eleanor (b. 1909). In 1922, Phebe Jane Stanley wrote her sister Nancy Turner in Nebraska: "Oh, Mr. King has a auto. He can drive up and down the road; of course he cannot get in the woods so it is not any good, only to haul from the shore that is something." The Model T's remains are still on Baker. (Right, LHD, Dale Robbins; below, GHMM.)

Eleanor King remembered going to Baker Island Schoolhouse until it closed and being terribly homesick when she moved to Southwest Harbor with mother Maud (left) and sister Edna. They returned to Baker at every opportunity, and many friends from Southwest Harbor came to visit. Below is a July 1922 advertisement for the only known shop on the island, probably Maud's. Eleanor married keeper Harold Robbins's (page 61) grandson. During this war period, young men were probably stationed on Baker in some capacity (watch duty and/or US Signal Corps). Nearly forgotten is young widower Harold E. Moore. His wife, Mildred Seeds, died in November 1917 after giving birth to daughter Leatha; bereft, Moore joined the Navy in December. He served on Baker for most of 1918 and died in December of influenza. (Left, LHD, Dale Robbins; below, Jesup Memorial Library.)

REST
NOW OPEN
AT
Baker Island, Maine
Until September 15

AFTERNOON TEAS SOUVENIRS
HOMEMADE CANDY SOFT DRINKS
FIR PILLOWS
SWEETGRASS BASKETS
Tel. Northeast Harbor 175-5

Joseph and Annie Muise experienced extremes of great joy and deep tragedy during their brief tenure on Baker Island, from 1930 to 1932. They arrived on the island in 1930, the year after Phebe Jane Stanley's death left the island uninhabited, with four children: Ronald, 10; Willard, 9; Madeline, 7; and newborn Adele. Annie's lightkeeper brother George Seavey had suggested Joseph enter the service. Having been abandoned in Southwest Harbor at age 12 by his widowed ship's captain father, Joseph knew hardship. The security of lighthouse keeping suited the young family, even after their Baker Island experiences. Keeper Muise proved to be meticulous, proud of keeping a pristine station his whole life. (Right, Muise family; below, LHD.)

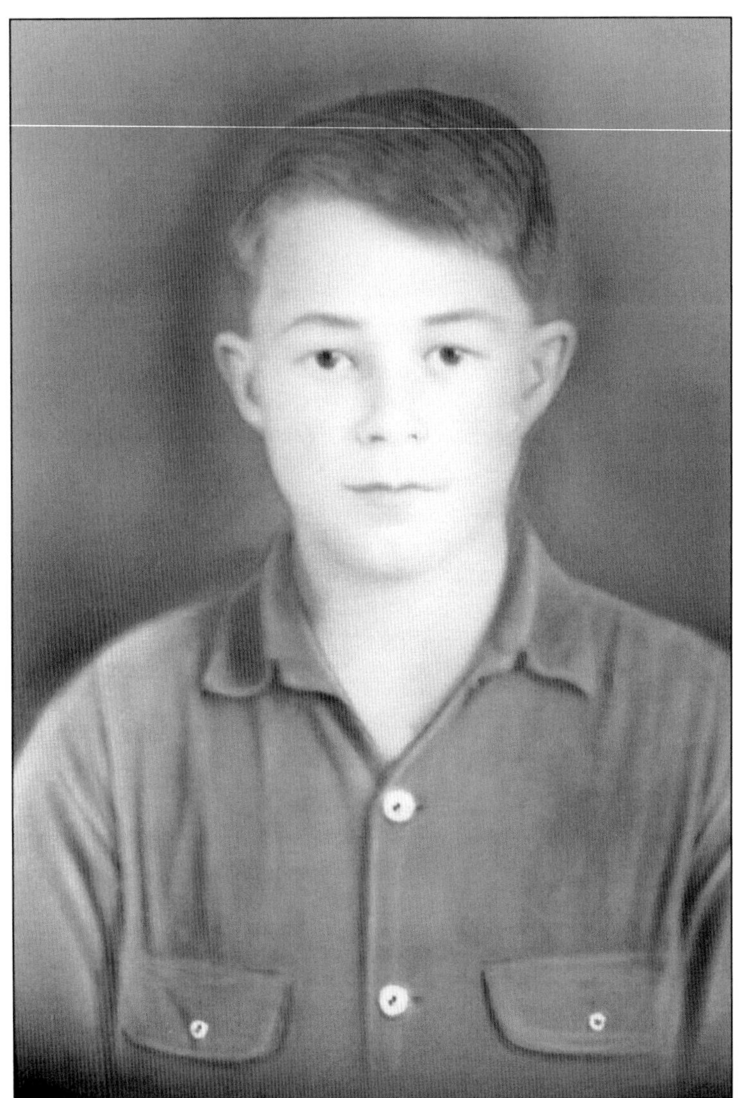

The school-aged Muise children spent from September to June in Southwest Harbor, returning to Baker Island each summer. It was in August 1932 that the Muise's oldest son, Ronald (left), died in an accident on a homemade raft. The newspaper account was dramatic but the diligent Muise simply recorded, without exceeding his daily logbook line: "Cleaned brass. Son Ronald was drownt 6:30 pm." Two days later, the following logbook entry appeared: "Went to SW Harbor to attend son furnal." (Left, Muise family; below, NARA.)

21	Sunday Station duties.
22	Went to N.E. Harbor for batteries.
23	Cleaned brass. Son Ronald was drownt 6:30 PM
24	Station duties
25	Went to S W Harbor to attend Son furnal.
26	Station duties
27	Cleand in tower in cellar.

Bereft, the Muises requested an immediate transfer. Before it was granted, however, their fifth child arrived. On a stormy November night, without anyone else to keep the light burning, Joseph Muise called the Islesford lifesaving station across the bar. The crew loaded his laboring wife onto a launch and started out across seven miles of chop, but the baby would not wait. Two miles from Southwest Harbor, baby Prudence was delivered into the wool peacoats of the surfmen. The *Bar Harbor Times* ran the headline, "Loses Race with Stork," on November 9, 1932. The once again understated line in the keeper's log reads: "Coast guard crew took Mrs to S.W.H. A baby girl was born." Pictured are Prudence (left) and Adele (right). Today, fortunate visitors to the Burnt Island Lighthouse visit with reenactors of the Muise family. (Right, Muise family; below, NARA.)

DEPARTMENT OF COMMERCE
LIGHTHOUSE SERVICE

JOURNAL OF LIGHT STATION AT Baker Island.

1932. MONTH	DAY	STATE WORK PERFORMED BY KEEPERS REGARDING UPKEEP OF STATION, AND RECORD OF IMPORTANT EVENTS, WEATHER CONDITIONS, ETC.
November.	1	Discovered light out at 1AM. o.k at 1 30 AM.
	2	Cleaned brass in service room.
	3	Cleaned out I.O.V lamps.
	4	Hauled oil cases to the shore.
	5	Went for mail. Cleaned woodwork
	6	Went to Manset for supplies.
	7	Washed woodwork in Wash room.
	8	Coast guard crew took Mrs to S.W.H. A Baby girl was born.

Frank Faulkingham relieved Muise in December 1932; his family followed. He and his wife, Olive, were from Jonesport; their children were Mina, 21; John Riley, 19; Myrtle, 16, and Lucille, 4. Faulkingham's service bridged the transition from US Lighthouse Service to US Coast Guard. He had served since 1919 but enlisted in the Coast Guard effective June 11, 1941, ranked at boatswain's mate first class. (Donna Madison.)

Frank Faulkingham's daughter Myrtle married Ken Sawyer of Manset, a keeper's son, and spent winters in the 1930s on Baker with her husband and parents. (Lucille was boarded off-island for school.) The marriage did not last, but the memories did. Kenny shared fantastic tales of winter on Baker. During World War II, Faulkingham served as "Chief" to young men on lookout station duty. He was very personable and became a local fixture. (Dana Sawyer.)

Pictured is the lighthouse tender *Lilac*. Frank Faulkingham's logs show the *Hibiscus* dropping off supplies regularly. It sometimes took five days to shuttle coal up from the shore. Empty oil cans were left at the landing for pickup. The keeper also noted observing the tender passing by en route to servicing nearby stations. (MDIHS.)

Frank Faulkingham was said to be "as fine a boatman as they come" and was a private captain to many after he retired. Ken Sawyer said of Olive, Faulkingham's wife, however: "I never seen a woman so scared of the water in all my life." She was rarely coaxed off Baker until she moved off permanently. Their son John Riley served in the Coast Guard with Sawyer during wartime. (Donna Madison.)

Several vehicles have been brought to Baker Island over the years. Capt. Vurney King's Model T is thought to be the first, and photographs from the 1940s reveal a Coast Guard Jeep. The date of the picture above must be between 1937 and 1957 (post flagpole and pre hyphen removal). The magnificent government Dodge Power Wagon, little changed from the 1940s into the 1960s, is no help establishing the date of the photograph below. (Above, GHMM; below, Brad Wetherll photograph, LHD.)

According to Wayne Holcomb's daughter Velna, he was the Coast Guard lighthouse keeper from at least 1944 until shortly after the end of World War II. His wife, Harriett (below), lived there with him. She reports that they both loved it and would have liked to stay and raise their family on Baker Island. (Both, Velna Holcomb Pennington.)

Sanford W. Colson married Phyllis Jarvis from Islesford in 1933 and was stationed at the Islesford Coast Guard station in 1940. He served as lighthouse keeper and/or substitute into the 1950s, as did Ernest Mathie. The two men painted the tower in October 1947, and other locals were hired for various work; Colson's brother-in-law Kenneth Jarvis worked with him in 1955, dismantling the light. The deactivation was protested with petitions (and intervention by Maine's senator). When reestablished in 1957, it was equipped with an automated lantern, ending the era of resident lightkeepers on Baker Island. By 1958, when the National Park Service acquired the light station compound, the hyphen had been removed and a fence installed to protect the tower and demarcate Coast Guard property. Colson died four years later, at age 50. (Above, GHMM; left, IHS.)

Six

School Days

Many Teachers but Few Scholars

Education was important to Hannah Gilley. A learned woman, she taught her children to read, write, and cipher. Early records are spotty, but at some point, a schoolteacher was hired. Possibly a live-in couple worked as housekeeper and schoolmaster. By 1857, Francis A. Thomas was paid $22 by the Town of Cranberry Isles to teach on Baker Island. Other early teachers included Julia A. Bunker (1858–1859), Inazella Robbins (1888), Nellie B. Mayo (1890), and Mary D. Morris (1893, 1895). At least two of these were daughters of lighthouse keepers, with siblings as pupils.

School was held in Elisha Gilley's summer kitchen until September 1896, when the Baker schoolhouse opened at a cost of $315. Six years prior, William P. Preble had written to lightkeeper Robbins, who did not pay the $2.99 poll tax because Cranberry Isles was not his family's home. It had come to Preble's attention that two scholars named Robbins attended school, although mother Eliza Robbins lived in Southwest Harbor; therefore, Preble insisted that Robbins owed $4.16.7 (calculated to tenths of a cent) per pupil. During subsequent years, annual costs of $195 ($120 for teachers, $75 for boarding) for several scholars was likely unpopular with frugal taxpayers. In 1897, the school had been open six months and was not yet paid off, yet already a ballot question asked "whether to continue School No. 5."

In March 1901, voters discontinued the school. Baker residents petitioned, requesting that the cost of boarding their two pupils elsewhere be spent operating the school and that any additional costs be "contributed by those interested." Baker Island did not have the 10 voters required to petition the board, but non-Baker allies signed as well. At a special meeting, it was decided to continue the school as before, fully town-funded.

Education and school funding typically elicit community controversy; the Cranberry Isles during this period were no exception. The political undercurrents remain unknown. The schoolhouse may have been built to stir up the government land ownership dispute or to solve it. It may have come from a straightforward desire to educate the children of Baker Island, or to pave the way for taxing the residents.

Mary Ann Carroll, Hannah Lurvey Gilley's niece, taught in Baker Island Schoolhouse in its first term (and others into 1905), writing: "I have a pleasant boarding place at Sam B. Gilley's. I have a nice new school house, a very small school; but I think the pupils will learn a good deal if nothing happens. The wreck [of the British Schooner *Atwood*] has taken the attention of the large boys some, and I hope I shall not be bothered with any more wrecks this winter." Carroll taught at other Cranberry Isles schools as well, and in a Great Cranberry Island report from 1893, she reflected: "These boys need more strict discipline. I tried to govern them with as little use of rod as possible. I think I may have 'spared the rod' too much. The law of love is to govern the world, but strict discipline must have its place, or the 'pearl' will be trampled underfoot." (GCIHS 2014.290.2045.)

Voters of Cranberry Isles approved a Baker Island schoolhouse, raising $100 in 1895; then in 1896, $15 for land and $200 for construction. In fall 1896, the *Bar Harbor Record* punned: "Bakers Island celebrates the opening of its first school-house. Bakers Island light is thus made brighter." Previously, school had been taught in the summer kitchen of the Elisha/Sam B. Gilley house. This picture was taken around 1991. (Photograph by Henry Grandgent.)

"The spring [1904] term of this school taught by Miss Viola F. Joy of Cranberry Isles, was good for so small a school . . . but needs more pupils to be of interest," reported Supt. Alonzo Bryant (grandson-in-law of William Gilley). Whether to continue the Baker school was a recurring debate almost annually from 1899 until 1919. Viola Joy, second from left, is pictured haying around 1910. She died in 1911. (SWHPL No. 11853.)

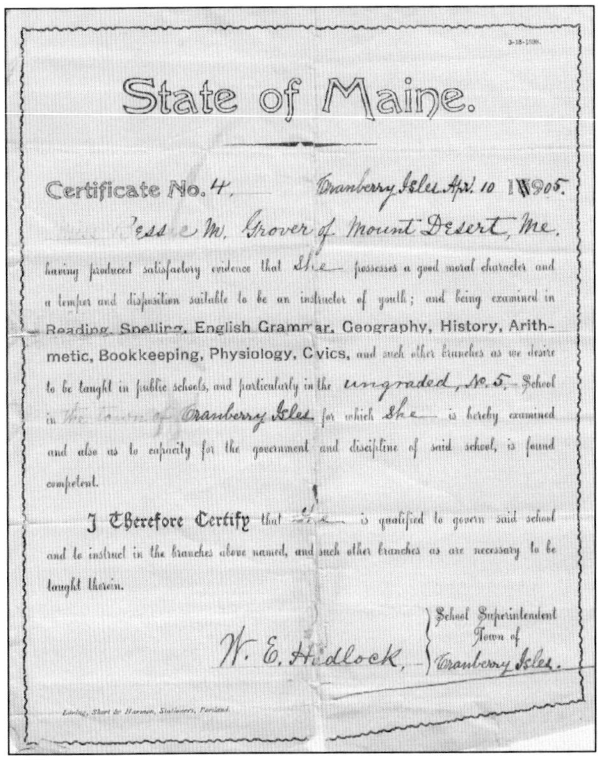

State of Maine.

Certificate No. 4, Cranberry Isles Apr. 10 1905.

Bessie M. Grover of Mount Desert, Me.

having produced satisfactory evidence that she possesses a good moral character and a temper and disposition suitable to be an instructor of youth; and being examined in Reading, Spelling, English Grammar, Geography, History, Arithmetic, Bookkeeping, Physiology, Civics, and such other branches as we desire to be taught in public schools, and particularly in the ungraded, No. 5, School in the Town of Cranberry Isles for which she is hereby examined and also as to capacity for the government and discipline of said school, is found competent.

I Therefore Certify that she is qualified to govern said school and to instruct in the branches above named, and such other branches as are necessary to be taught therein.

W. E. Hadlock, School Superintendent Town of Cranberry Isles.

Loring, Short & Harmon, Stationers, Portland.

Bessie M. Grover received approval to teach on Baker in the spring of 1905, following a term by Laura Nelson. Grover stayed for the fall of 1905, receiving a raise from $30 to $40 for 10-week terms. For boarding, an island resident could earn $2.50 per week, and the women took turns boarding teachers, as the men did serving as school agent for District No. 5. During this time, George Smith courted Grover by rowboat. They married and remained in their hometown, Otter Creek, thereafter. Bessie Grover was descended from James Richardson, who, contrary to common belief, was the first European to permanently settle Mount Desert Island. Richardson remained, whereas Abraham Somes returned to Massachusetts before moving back to Somesville (or Richardsonville, as it might have been named). (Both, Paula Richardson Gannon.)

For the winter term of 1906, teacher Edna Campbell (above left, with her sister Ada) was paid $40. Sam B. Gilley was paid $25 for board, and fuel was $3. That spring's report read: "The school on Bakers Island has but two pupils living there now, with the prospect that only one of them will attend the school the coming year." After that, 16-year-old pupils Gerald Stanley and Leona Gilley went fishing and to school on Islesford, respectively, and the Baker Island Schoolhouse closed until the fall of 1911 with the arrival of teacher Abbie Hanna. Edna Campbell was the granddaughter of Benjamin and Almina (Gilley) Campbell and great-granddaughter of William and Hannah Gilley. She is pictured below, at left, with Eunice Coggins (center) and sister Ada Campbell (right). Edna Campbell married George Hadlock and had four sons. (Both, IHS.)

In January 1911, Vera Eunice Cole arrived on Baker Island. She was the new teacher and also the niece of keeper George Connors's new bride. Cole stayed with her aunt Mary and taught her cousin Gussie Moore. She confessed later that she was happy after her first term to board with Phebe Jane Stanley, who baked pies and cookies. Pictured at the lightkeeper's quarters are, from left to right, (first row) Gussie Moore and Leah Connors; (second row) Vera Cole and Mary Cole Moore Connors. Note Gussie's commentary on the photograph: "Sure, and those were happy days! Baker Island." This period was bustling on Baker Island. The extended Connors-Moore family brought a social life that may have been waning. Connections were developed among rusticators, teachers, and residents, on Baker and across the bar. (Mildred Chalmers.)

Above is the only known photograph of the Baker Island Schoolhouse in session. From left to right are teacher Vera Cole with Leroy Spurling and Leah Connors (both about eight), and Gussie Moore (about 14). Below is an image of the schoolhouse interior as it appears today, with less serious summer term students in 1998. They are, from left to right, Baker residents Jalana Pearson Sloatman, Amadea Cesari, Xander Cesari (front), and Henry Cesari. The holes in the slate, according to Leona Gilley, were made by an island cow named Nuisance. Baker childhood has changed little: exploring fairy houses, skipping stones, and tracking elusive mink. Games of imagination include the challenge of creating objects using whatever washes up. There are card games and endless reading. Winter pastimes included sliding and pond skating. The only new addition is probably quidditch. (Above, Laurie Rowen; below, Henry Kolm.)

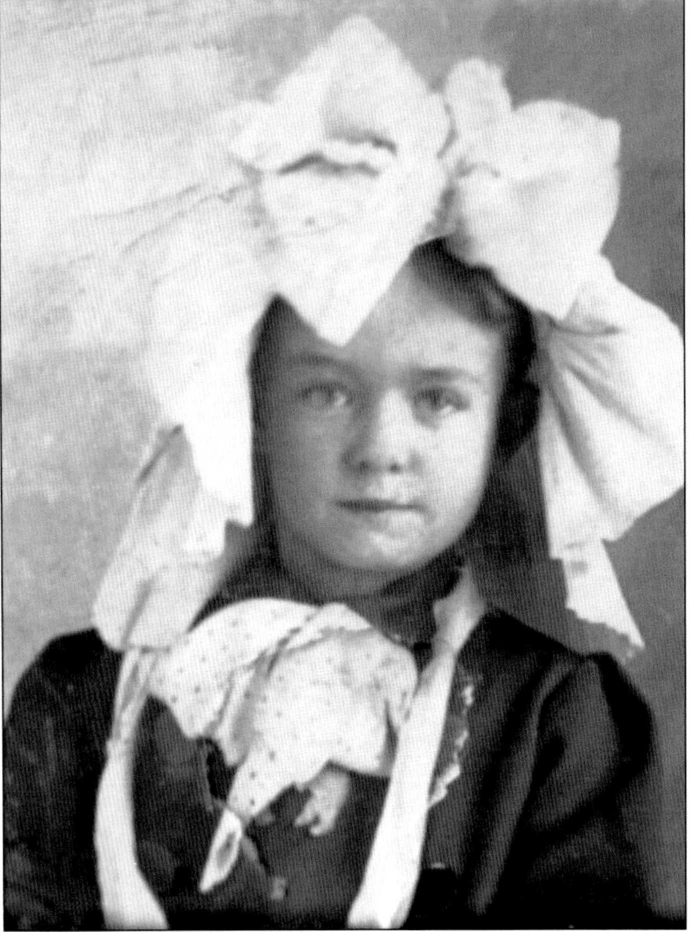

Vera Cole worked during the summer for a family on Mount Desert Island. The bustling society life must have provided a dramatic contrast to off-season Baker Island. This photograph of Cole may have been taken near the Claremont Hotel, looking up Somes Sound, with her summer "charges." At left, Roy Spurling appears to have been dressed up by his classmates (page 85). In a reverse of the usual, Roy and his sister Thelma boarded on Baker for school. Little is known except that their father, Everett "Jiggle" Spurling, lived with Sam B. Gilley for some time before his marriage to Georgia Spofford. (Above, Laurie Rowan; left, Mildred Chalmers.)

Six-year-old Ralph Demmons's widowed mother, Gertrude "Gerty," taught on Baker Island in the winter of 1913. She only taught one term, however, and in August was married to Gussie Moore's brother Russell. At some point, Russell served at the Coast Guard station across the bar; his adopted son Ralph joined the Coast Guard as well. Ralph served at Brant Rock and Point Allerton Stations in Massachusetts, then Mount Desert Rock in the late 1940s. Below is a picture of Russell and Gerty Moore with the Hurd family, the in-laws of Mary Cole's sister Olive. Gerty is at center, with her son Ralph in front and Russell next to her. (Both, Mildred Chalmers.)

Teacher Sara Mayo (later Chapman) described her 1914 journey to Baker via train to the Bar Harbor Ferry, the buckboard stage to Seal Harbor, and a boat to Islesford. With the tide too high to cross the bar, she wrote that US Life-Saving Service captain Stanley told her "I could stay at the Station and I would be just as safe as I would be at home . . . curled up in a big soft leather chair with a box of chocolates at my disposal. Wasn't that solid comfort? . . . If he wasn't married and was a little younger I should have fallen in love with him . . . he was fine, just gentlemanly and nice all through." The eight men were "every one as nice as could be . . . up in the watch tower I helped a fellow (married ha'ah') watch." At left, Sara poses with her younger siblings. (Both, Kenneth Chapman.)

Sara Mayo (right) also wrote home: "I think there are five families in all here, all close together. I only have three scholars and the cutest little school house. I am sure I am going to like here, still I have a feeling that I would be glad to go home when the term is over." Ina Jordan, below, taught on Baker Island for the fall terms in 1913 and 1914. Other teachers included Luella Tufts, Estella B. Dyer, Lovisa Hanson, Sadie Doyen, Marguerite Littlefield, Louise Johnson, Hattie Hunter, Louise Morris, Alice L. Ames, Annie F. Bodge, Anna Smith, and Agnes Hall. Agnes Hall told her grandson it was fortunate she could run because the half dozen young men stationed there on watch duty were awfully glad to have a single woman on the island. (Right, Kenneth Chapman; below, Mildred Chalmers.)

In Jennie A. Stanley's last term as superintendent of Cranberry Isles schools, she somewhat defensively reported: "It was voted . . . to continue the Baker Island school for the spring term, 1916, and to determine later whether a school should or should not be supported there by the town in the fall . . . the problem was settled . . . when it was decided the only intelligent way out of this difficulty was to have a school at Baker Island subject to the same privileges as the other schools in town. Those who will remember the old verse 'Do unto others as you would that they should do to you,' etc., will not censure us for taking this stand on the question." After that, Velma Teele, pictured here, became superintendent. The Baker Island Schoolhouse closed its doors forever around 1919. (IHS.)

Seven

Life on Baker

Fishing, Hunting, Harvest, and Lore

On Baker Island, the sound of surf, taste of salt, and feel of the tides are ubiquitous. The sea permeates all. Life is fishing, boats, surf, storms, and shipwrecks.

Harvard president Charles W. Eliot wrote: "Boys who become good boatmen must have had an admirable training in alertness, prompt decision, resource in emergencies, and courageous steadiness in difficulties and dangers . . . taught by these struggles with nature to be vigilant, patient, self-reliant, and brave." (Gilley girls, like Leona, were sailors, too!)

Even now, Baker summer residents experience challenges demanding resourcefulness and flexibility, like inability to land safely for days (both coming on and getting off Baker), limited supplies, and hauling provisions uphill from the landing. But while chores were plentiful, so was food. It was said that during an especially hard winter, the Gilleys provided food for folks in Southwest Harbor from their own excess stores.

Alfred Stanley reflected on his Baker upbringing in a 1907 Tacoma crashed economy: "I guess I can hard time as well as the rest so I don't worry over it much . . . I wish I had a farm down near the beach I tell you he is the man that is well off if he only knew it."

Later he said, "There's lots of stories. Mother used to sing some of them." As old women, Phebe Jane Stanley and her sisters shared ballads of pirates, mourning lost sailors, and whaling expeditions, some of which appear in *Minstrelsy of Maine*, 1925.

Great stories need not necessarily be true. There are at least two Baker Island versions of one story involving a British frigate whose captain and 12 crewmembers landed on Baker in 1814. They killed half the stock, providing a note on the British crown as compensation, then ordered William Gilley to pilot the ship into Norwood's Cove. Using savvy navigation, he anchored the enemy ship where it would flounder at low tide. On shore, a few patriots marched the vanquished crew to Bangor. "That's the Battle of Norwood's Cove, where your great great great great grandfather captured a British battleship," finished Alfred. Even with historical variations, William Gilley has never before—off Baker Island—been credited with single-handedly defeating the *Tenedos*.

The Gilleys built fish houses on the northern shore of Baker Island, pictured here sometime after 1900. The sheltered coves on both sides of the bar were bountiful; lobsters were easily gathered, and herring and other fish netted for smoking. These fish houses may have been clubhouses of sorts, where fishermen spent time visiting. Subjected to punishing conditions, the shore structures were short-lived and few photographs remain. (ANP.)

Elisha Gilley is seen here mending nets. The Gilleys had a weir down by the bar, and nets required maintenance. One way to protect them was to dip them in a cauldron of hot tar, which strengthened the twine and made the nets impervious to saltwater. Tar streaks can still be seen at the landing on Baker Island, where this photograph was taken. When lobster fishing became lucrative, other tasks emerged—bait bags and heads were knitted for lobster traps, and latch buttons and claw pegs whittled. (ANP.)

The men of Baker Island were cod fishermen in the 19th century. Lobster could be gathered in the shallows but was smashed for the hens. "Lobstering" replaced "codfishing" on the 1900 census. Above is a wet-well lobster smack, with an open pound in the hull. The Gilleys would keep their catch in submerged crates until it was transferred into the hold of a smack, which arrived offshore buying lobster. The smacks also carried provisions to sell to islanders: drums of staples, sides of pork, biscuits, etc. Leona Gilley did not like fish, and her father, Sam B., would buy meat to hold them over until he had an animal to kill and store outdoors over winter. Her uncle Sam Gilley, pictured below around 1894, lobstered off Gilley Beach; Baker Island can be seen behind him. (Above, photograph by W.H. Ballard, MDIHS; below, ANP.)

Maine carefully manages its lobster fishery, protecting lobsters under 3.5 inches and over five (eye socket to back of shell), as well as egg-bearing females, which are marked with a notched tail and released. Stefanie Alley, pictured at left in 2013, fishes off Baker Island in the fishing vessel *Ashley n Lucy*. This lobster was too large to get into a trap but clung to the outside of it as Alley pulled it up. Hopefully, it is creeping off Baker still, producing thousands of larvae each season. Alley takes passengers aboard for lobster boat tours. Below is Henry Grandgent, descendant of Harvard professor Charles H. Grandgent. He works mostly for summer residents in the Cranberries, performing maintenance and master traditional carpentry. Grandgent's Baker escapades span half a century, and he is responsible for many hours of island maintenance. (Left, Stefanie Alley; below, KOBI.)

In August 1955, Capt. Lyndon "Tud" Bunker (on left at right) was off Baker Island aboard John L. Saltonstall's 32-foot cabin cruiser *Thetis*. She was rammed below the waterline about three feet from the bow (below), and Captain Bunker harpooned a 1,000-pound shark (not necessarily in that order). The shark was shot and killed by a boat coming to their rescue. One of its teeth was sent to Henry B. Bigelow of the Museum of Comparative Zoology at Harvard College, who identified it as a *Carcharodon carcharias*, or great white shark. Saltonstall received great publicity over the event back home in Boston. (Both, GCIHS 1000.28.404.)

In June 1973, unable to resist "a long-period swell pushing overhead peelers onto the submerged granite shelf," Jay Speakman anchored his lobster boat and hopped overboard, without a wetsuit, to surf the northeast point of Baker Island. In his words, he "set up to shoulder-hop a set wave and was soon fading into a long head-high peeler, which I managed to ride all the way around the point, finally kicking out in the cove." The Speakman brothers, Jay and Christopher, are descendants of locals and grew up summering in the Cranberry Isles but also lived in Maui, where they developed expert surfing skills. Christopher is a professional photographer, and both brothers still return to the area with cameras and surfboards. Above, Jay surfs the northeast point; below, Chris is at Sand Beach Cove. Both images are from 1983. (Both, Christopher Speakman.)

When Alfred Stanley moved west, "gunning" and eating seabirds still brought great delight, despite the reactions of his roommates to the smell. Kenny Sawyer (below) also loved hunting. He lauded the tenacity of Frank Faulkingham's Chesapeake Bay retriever Tootles (right): "It was five below one morning . . . the ducks all come in, bundled up tight. I seen them set their wings, and fly up, and I let go with both barrels. I don't know how many sea ducks was in the water, but that dog she went out 13 or 14 times. And she'd ice up before she get back out . . . you been out there when a thumper comes up—you seen that? We'd watch, and when three big ones comes, we'd say 'let her go,' cause then there'd be three small ones." (Right, photograph by Lyle Stepanek, Nancy Stepanek Rosburg; below, Dana Sawyer.)

Kenny Sawyer and Frank Faulkingham put up a winter's hay for a cow using hand scythes as pictured below with Sam and George Gilley. More challenging, Sawyer recalled, was getting a bull onto the island to service her every year. He described one occasion when they were rowing one out and discovered the bull was "all lousy. . . . We didn't have no lice on Baker, and we didn't want 'em. So we pushed that bull overboard and let him swim ashore. We had such a pretty heifer waiting, we knew he'd come along. And he weren't so lousy when he come ashore. He did good work for a few days and earned his ride home." Sawyer also described butchering hogs and calves and corning spare ribs, cod, and beef. (Left, photograph by Lyle Stepanek, Nancy Stepanek Rosburg; below, ANP.)

Even with Islesford an "isles' ford" away, isolation was a reality and self-reliance a necessity. Joseph and William Gilley planted many apple trees, some of which survive. Vegetables were grown in quantity, a dairy cow was almost always in residence, and rhubarb still abounds. Many varieties of berries were gathered and put up in jars, and bushels of root cellar crops were stored packed in sand. These photographs are both dated around the 1940s, revealing the rapid rate of decay claiming the original Gilley homestead. Given that date, the unidentified young lady below must be a keeper's daughter or a visitor. Leona Gilley told stories of Nuisance, an island cow. Nuisance would chew the fishermen's oilskins off the laundry lines and would wander into any building she liked. It was Nuisance, Leona said, who rammed the matched pairs of holes in the schoolhouse slate chalkboard. (Both, ANP.)

Sailing has long been a way of life in the Acadia region, for trade and transportation but also sport. Baker Island is a favorite destination for day trips; sailors and yachtsmen sometimes anchor offshore and overnight aboard. Baker is used as a mark in regattas. The Seal Harbor Yacht Club and the Northeast Harbor Fleet both maintain moorings off the landing. Leona Gilley had her own sailboat. This photograph was taken around 1916. (Gail M. Carr.)

Groups of swimmers are not often seen at Baker's Landing. In this photograph, taken around 1938 at high tide, the top of the boat rails are visible; in the distance, Green Nubble emerges near the center of the bar. A 1909 court ruling specified that the "boat landing as it exists shall be forever kept open and used in common by the Government and those interested in the island for landing purposes." (ANP.)

Eight

The Dance Floor

Rusticators, Intellectuals, and Artists

The Mount Desert Island region was discovered as a summer destination beginning around 1844, when Thomas Cole of the Hudson Valley School visited and painted its landscape. This drew many literally to Eden (as Bar Harbor was named): "We are still in Eden; the wall that shuts us out of the garden is our own ignorance and folly," Cole wrote in *American Monthly* magazine in 1836. "May we at times turn from the ordinary pursuits of life to the pure enjoyment of rural nature; which is in the soul like a fountain of cool waters to way-worn travelers." An artistic period of "romantic primitivism" naturally brought forth "rusticators." The desire to recapture the simplicity of the outdoors—to cleanse the spirit—sent artists working plein air and socialites motoring over the water to hike across Baker Island and picnic on the pink granite expanse known as the Dance Floor. Some even transported victrolas—or musicians—and danced giddily in the ocean spray. Pioneers in the medical field, clergy, and creative souls were drawn to the natural beauty of Acadia, along with writers and poets, photographers and painters. Some were academics: Harvard president Charles W. Eliot, who wrote about John Gilley, adored the region and introduced it to friends including professor Charles H. Grandgent. Wealthy philanthropists with names like Astor, Ford, and Rockefeller had shingled "cottages" built overlooking harbors.

Henry Wadsworth Longfellow's daughter Annie Allegra and her husband, Joseph Thorp Jr., summered on Greenings Island. They so enjoyed Baker that they purchased the Dance Floor from Sam Gilley in 1909.

Several rusticators who wrote extensively about the Cranberry Isles are liberally quoted here. William O. Sawtelle, historian, and Dr. Vincent Bowditch, physician, were two learned gentlemen who showed a long-term commitment to the people and history of the Cranberry Isles. Sawtelle carried out research, documentation, and preservation; Dr. Bowditch kept detailed journals over his 34 years of visits. These accounts help paint vibrant images of the landscape of Baker Island as it appeared—and events as they occurred—at the time. As valuable perhaps, the erudite patois of the writers, coupled with images of their cultured contemporaries, places one in their midst.

Joseph and Anne Allegra Longfellow Thorp's granddaughter Frances Wetherell recalls family visits to the Dance Floor. One spring, they found that a tremendous storm had shifted rocks enough to alter, and diminish, the surface. The only sign they ever posted asked visitors not to build fires. "Then we came out one day to find that it had been used for firewood, and that was that." There were five Thorp daughters: Alice, Amelia, Erica, Anne, and Priscilla. The Dance Floor is now owned by the family in the form of the Greenings Island Trust. On a 1910 outing (left), lounging in the bow, is probably Alice Allegra. The Thorps had a launch called the *Rosemary*. (Both, NPS Longfellow House–Washington's Headquarters National Historic Site, Archives No. 1002-9-4-360 [left] and No. 1002-9-4-361 [below].)

One of the five Thorp daughters, Anne (1894–1977) was lifelong friends with keeper George Connors's stepdaughter Gussie Moore (page 67); above, Anne is pictured on a Dance Floor outing with family members (possibly the Moore family) in 1959. Below, the middy-clad Thorps enjoy a view around 1910. On the left are parents Joseph Thorp Jr. and Anne Allegra Longfellow Thorp. Anne Longfellow Thorp is likely at far right. (Above, Mildred Chalmers; below, NPS Longfellow House–Washington's Headquarters National Historic Site Archives No. 1002-9-4-362.)

Dr. Charles and Abigail Seelye Scudder of Boston were summer visitors starting around 1898. Dr. Scudder was chief surgeon at Massachusetts General Hospital. Extended family has summered in the area since. Their granddaughter Gail M. Carr recalls that they "often rowed out to the islands, the men in their jackets and ties and the ladies in long skirts, to picnic. My grandfather and great-uncle even used to row out to Mt. Desert Rock!" Pictured above around 1907 is her mother, Hilda Chapin Scudder, who became a famous sculptor (see page 12). Below, around 1905, two young mariners (possibly James and William Dana) float toy boats in tidal pools. (Above, Gail M. Carr; below, Dana family collection, Willis family.)

In 2001, the Downeast Dance swing dancing group came to take a turn around the famous Dance Floor. Cranberry Isles residents escorted the dancers and documented the event; most notably, artist Wini Smart created a painting on the spot called *Dancing on the Rocks*. Leona Gilley remembered the Baker Island children playing on what they called the Dance Hall, complete with audience seats, but ironically, they never learned to dance. "We had no place to learn, growing up on Baker." Some might disagree! (Both, Wini Smart.)

Baker's serenity provided respite from the dizzying whirl of summer society on Mount Desert. In 1896, Dr. Vincent Bowditch, who founded a tuberculosis sanatorium in Sharon, Massachusetts, recognized the renewal offered by the Dance Floor. "After lunch we all walked down to the superb red granite rocks on the shore. They lie like great ruins of Druidial temples, the relics of some titanic race. As the surf came rolling in, the delicious sea breeze filling our lungs with oxygen, mere existence seemed a delight. For a long time I lay flat on my back and let sun and air pour over me." Pictured above are Buckman family members and friends in 1919. At left, Caroline Bristol Dana is pictured in mourning attire, perhaps grieving the 1907 death of her mother. (Above, SWHPL No. 8780; left, Dana family collection, Willis family.)

Eileen Rockefeller Growald recalls, "When I was a child my parents took the six of us to Bakers Island for picnics on the dancing rocks. I remember the walk seeming to be long, as we all helped carry baskets and thermoses for our picnic lunch. But the excitement of arriving at those large expanses of pink granite was worth the effort! My mother used to take a dip before lunch in the ocean right off the rocks. We children looked in tide pools and explored the cracks and caves among the rocks. It remains a favorite picnic spot today." Above, Eileen Growald is pictured in 2007. Below are her sons Adam and Danny in August 1990, fifth-generation Dance Floor Rockefellers. (Both, Eileen Growald.)

Dr. Vincent Bowditch's detailed entry of August 13, 1913, reads, "Yesterday we suddenly decided to take supper at Baker's Island as the weather seemed propitious . . . we started arriving about 4:45 and springing from the boat from the bow. Thinking Scotty was going to pull me by the hand as he stood on the shore, I missed my mark and went in over both shoes which was a good beginning for a picnic! Animal heat & a walk over the island and when on the rocks by cooking 'hash' and at the same time warming my feet at the alcohol burner, I was soon dry. The moon (not full) soon appeared above us toward sunset. . . . Lovely sail home in the moonlight. Landed on the rocks about 8:00 p.m." (Both, ANP.)

Helen Mayo August 1, 1911
Lawrence Shaw Mayo
C. Scott White Aug 2
Nina White

cheerily

A merry song, a chorus brave,
And yet a sigh regret
For roses sweet, in woodland lanes
Ah, love can ne'er forget!
Edward Mac Dowell

Baker's Island
Aug. 4th

Many of Dr. Vincent Bowditch's friends were artists, including C. Scott White and his wife, Nina. He refers, on visits to Baker Island, to leaving Scotty at the shore to sketch the fish houses. The resultant sketch can be found in White's body of work. Above is a page from Bowditch's journal, showing a White sketch and whimsical tune jotted out by Lawrence Shaw Mayo with an Edward Mac Dowell verse. *The Islesford Journals*, transcribed and printed in four volumes by Hugh Dwelley, are available through the Islesford Historical Society. Below, members of a Dana family outing explore tidal pools. Somehow their hats remain in place. (Above, IHS; below, Dana family collection, Willis family.)

Baker Island's beauty has long inspired artists in many media. Photography was quite popular in the Dana family, and at least one camera was present for many outings. Above, Caroline Bristol Dana has captured another photographer using a box camera. Below is a view of the Islesford Station from the northwest side of Baker taken by Islesford resident, postmaster, and artist Joy Sprague. (Above, Dana family collection, Willis family; below, Joy Sprague.)

Photographer and writer LaRue Striker traveled to Baker Island frequently, and it is well represented in her work. This photograph was taken from the watchtower past the tower. The fence dates it post-1958; the watchtower, pre-1960s. (MDIHS.)

This model of Baker Island Lighthouse was built around 1950 and donated to Great Harbor Maritime Museum in Northeast Harbor. The lighthouse and wooden keeper's house have electric lights, and a metal Lionel train set tower represents the watchtower. Local museums have displayed this piece and would like to give credit to the builder, pictured here; unfortunately, his identity is currently unknown. (GHMM.)

Wini Smart was a noted Great Cranberry Island artist who painted extensively in the region and found inspiration on Baker Island. Her art captures Baker's spirit, in fog and sunshine. Her works include dancing on the rocks, the lighthouse amidst spruce and mist, and the Wyethesque Elisha Gilley house. A common medium was watercolor as well as pastels, although Smart used various methods; pictured above is a rare early sketch. Her daughter Gail Cleveland is an artist as well. At left, island resident and budding artist Jalana Pearson Sloatman is entranced by the process of artist John Wagner around 1994. (Above, Fred Quackenbush and Jim and Cessie Sawyer; left, Bettina Pearson and David Sloatman.)

Nine

Stewardship

Decline and Reclamation

In the early 19th century, the Gilleys transformed forest to pastures, farmland, and even a small quarry. By century's end, agricultural activity dramatically decreased. Fields were overgrown with thickets and encroaching spruce. Vacated by 1920, farm buildings began irreversible deterioration.

With the lighthouse came highly disciplined and organized keepers. Their diligent maintenance of all structures under their care continued until 1955. Once abandoned, these buildings also decayed quickly, with several collapsing. In 1958, Acadia National Park acquired the 10-acre light station, except the tower on a 20-by-20-foot plot. The US Coast Guard recognized the threat posed by unchecked vegetation; the property transfer stipulated that "no construction or natural growth be allowed on the ten acres that might obscure the light," visible for 11 miles at the time. However—perhaps due to procedural, budgetary, and political constraints—this condition was not upheld, even after land acquisitions in 1966 and 1983 gave the park ownership of most of the island and responsibility for its management.

In 1987, a Coast Guard helicopter landed and modern lighthouse treatment—sandblasting with "black beauty"—was inflicted on the 132-year-old tower, accelerating its decay. In 1988, the entire light station was listed in the National Register of Historic Places, forever preventing such treatment. Acadia's 2011 acquisition of the tower itself carried another stipulation—the National Park Service must maintain the tower that holds the Coast Guard's lantern.

Residents Kathleen and Ron Pearson arrived in the 1960s followed by Elizabeth and Henry Kolm. Both families took a keen interest in stewardship. They kept paths open and trash cleaned up as best they could by hand and without park collaboration.

In 2004, Elizabeth Kolm's daughter Cornelia (the author) and Henry Grandgent (equipped with a 1930s Rosamund Lord painting for reference) tentatively entered park headquarters asking for, and offering, help. They were met with open arms. Within weeks, Henry Kolm, Henry Grandgent, and John Cesari were given training, safety equipment, use of the barn, and encouragement. That fall, they landed a vintage Gravely sulky tractor and other equipment, launching a new era of Baker stewardship. This mutually beneficial partnership and effective collaboration with other organizations has yielded tremendous results.

Baker's offshore environment is typically harsh. Once left vacant, buildings showed immediate signs of neglect. The government boathouse was well maintained while there was a keeper. These pictures, taken around 1958 and in the 1970s, show rapid deterioration and the impending doom of the structure. Chris and Jay Speakman were two of the last to observe the boathouse still standing, while fishing in the 1970s. The doors had fallen off, and in a storm the previous night, a northeast wind had inflated the building and literally blown it apart. (Above, NARA; below, ANP.)

By the 1980s, Main Street was a one-lane footpath through thorny bushes. Visitors, arms overhead, were snagged, scratched, and soaked (in dew or fog). Above, Paul Growald and son Adam enter the "chute" in 1990. Vegetation enveloping buildings created shade, trapping moisture. Spruce trees thrived, and visitors walking to the Dance Floor often missed sight of the tower less than 200 feet away. Time took its toll on the cemetery as headstones tipped over, with several breaking. Sod besieged small markers and downed stones, its moisture hastening degradation. It appeared Baker Island was trying to erase its past by swallowing the plot. (Above, Eileen Rockefeller Growald; below, Henry Grandgent.)

In 2009, KOBI facilitated a restoration of the cemetery spearheaded by Hugh Dwelley and Islesford Historical Society. After extensive preparation, H.W. Dunn and Son of Ellsworth, KOBI volunteers, and island descendants tackled the project. It was almost finished in one day. Above, from left to right, Hugh Dwelley, Dale Hadlock, Gerry Fernald, and Ralph Stanley flank three workers from Dunn in the foreground. At left, boatbuilder Ralph W. Stanley, who placed a marker for his uncle Bert that day, takes a breather to tell some tales. (Both, KOBI.)

The August 2012 photograph above shows the restored cemetery planted with mums. Each year, the stones are cleared of lichen and inspected and the grass is trimmed without nicking the soft marble. In 2017, the headstone of Charles A. Gilley fell and cracked in two, a reminder of the tough environment of the northern bluff. Below, the author tends to the cemetery in 2012, a favorite task during which she can often be heard chatting away "to her peeps." (Both, KOBI.)

Baker is something of a catcher's mitt, scooping up drifting detritus. Debris deposited by storms rests over 100 feet above the high tide line. Routine communal efforts keep the landing and Dance Floor picked up, but not until 2011 with KOBI's Baker Island Shoreline Cleanup Initiative was a whole island/all trash effort launched. Logistical challenges and the volume of trash created a major undertaking. Volunteers from Clean Waters Clean Shores (below), transported by the Bar Harbor Whale Watch Company, joined the efforts already made by KOBI to accomplish a major cleanup of the more remote areas. Day-trippers, residents, and National Park Service personnel have all pitched in on this never-ending task. (Both, KOBI.)

Hiking across the island, breaking down three lobster traps, and packing them to the landing takes almost two hours. To date, hundreds of buoys, dozens of bags of trash, and over 100 "ghost traps" have been removed. This required a substantial number of volunteer hours. Access is difficult with no dock and a rocky landing. Acadia utilized three boats and 11 employees to transport over a ton of staged material. While each spring finds trash deposited, the annual cleanup is now easier. Private boats may remove trash; removing fishing gear, artifacts, or anything else from Baker is illegal. Special dispensation was granted to KOBI by the Department of Marine Resources to allow for "molestation of fishing gear," which is a crime. (Both, KOBI.)

Reclaiming fields began with KOBI's John Cesari riding a Gravely two-wheeled tractor behind a 30-inch brush mower capable of chopping small trees. At that time, no barge operators would land on Baker; Henry Grandgent landed in 2004 using a small boat pushing a swim float. A corroded wire on the spark plug kept the Gravely from starting as the tide rose—it was repaired in the nick of time. It mowed several acres that first year. The slightly newer Kubota tractor below has proven invaluable. In 2008, it was barged to Islesford, then driven by Cesari across the bar on a pre-scouted and timed course during low tide. The crossing took longer than planned, which caused an unscheduled overnight on Green Nubble. The tractor's remarkable log-skidding capacity has impressed National Park Service crews, and visitors frequently remark on the granite block lashed to the front for weight. (Both, KOBI.)

Mowing is primarily for fire prevention and returning fields to a period of historical significance. Other benefits include improved building health and easier accessibility for visitors (and less mosquito habitat). As the fields are expanded, hay is gathered (above in 2013) for native mulch and seed mix, encouraging growth. Hay is also used to restore burn sites. When KOBI and the National Park Service started controlled burn projects, a helicopter landing site was designated and mowed. It has been mowed each year since, out of sequence with the rest of the cutting, so it clearly contrasts for visibility from the air. In August 2012, a hiker was injured and Life Flight was summoned, using the established landing area for the first time. (Both, KOBI.)

The 2007 photograph above shows the severely overgrown lighthouse compound. Since then, controlled burns have been used on Baker for over a decade. Initially to burn brush from blowdowns, the scope and size have increased. In 2010, the park decided to cut and burn trees around the structures for fire protection, with the additional benefits of improved building health and restoration of historic vistas. Logistically challenging, there were months of extensive preparation for a two-week work period in 2012. Shown at the ready below, a crew of National Park Service fire personnel, with mountains of gear, was transported by the College of the Atlantic. Acadia Fire Management had already been prepping and landed over a ton of drinking water (unavailable on the island) along with pumps, tanks, and other supplies. (Both, KOBI.)

The initial plan had been to build piles and burn them later, but the concentration of material was too dense. On day two, conditions were evaluated, burn sites selected, and fires lit. While crews hauled much material by hand, production was dramatically increased by KOBI's John Cesari skidding logs for the entire period (above in 2012). Over 300 trees were cut, with results shown below. This project received national recognition for the National Park Service—the 2012 Fuels and Ecology Award in Promoting Fire-Adapted Human Communities. This allowed for a return the following year, when a barge was utilized to land equipment and supplies. Cesari returned with a larger tractor, again increasing production. Minimal site restoration was needed on both projects. Reactions from visitors were overwhelmingly positive. (Above, Conor Laffey; below, NPS.)

The photograph above shows the barn after Acadia's Maintenance Division restored it in 2011. Work included foundation, flooring, siding, painting, and building a ramp for easier storage of equipment. This building houses KOBI equipment and also Acadia Fire Management tools. During controlled burns it is used as a command post. It has been well preserved as a valuable resource. The area has been cleared for both fire protection and building health. Residents Cesari (left) and David Sloatman (right) can be seen at work rebuilding the island trailer. The tower (below) is at the other end of the spectrum. While structurally sound, it needs extensive repair, as detailed in a 2008 condition report. The project will require a Herculean effort by many organizations and take substantial time to complete. (Both, KOBI.)

The sweeping historic photograph above dates from the 1880s. The schoolhouse had not been built, but it appears that William Stanley's was under way. The remains of the original rubblestone keeper's house are visible, and the government barn was in use, predating 1905 facilities to the southwest. This period marked the peak of Baker Island's population, when it sustained over two dozen residents in five households. This community of farmer-fishermen required a symbiotic relationship as stewards of their environment, depending upon the resources provided by land and sea. These images document the extensive agriculture and aquaculture practiced by the Gilleys and the results of their labor. While this unique way of life is long past, Baker Island's preservation helps to keep a piece of history alive. The image below is from around 1905. (Above, NARA; below, Willis family.)

BIBLIOGRAPHY

Annual Report of the Municipal Officers of the Town of Cranberry Isles, Maine. 1831–present.

Bowditch, Dr. Vincent Y. *The Islesford Journals* vol. I–IV. (transcribed by Hugh L. Dwelley). Islesford, ME: The Islesford Historical Society, 1990–1995.

Clifford, J. Candace and Mary Louise. *Maine Lighthouses: Documentation of their Past.* Alexandria, VA: Cypress Communications, 2005.

Eckstrom, Fannie H. and M.W. Smyth, eds. *Minstrelsy of Maine: Folk-Songs and Ballads of the Woods and the Coast.* Cambridge, MA: The Riverside Press, 1927.

Eliot, Charles W. *John Gilley, Maine Farmer and Fisherman.* Boston, MA: American Unitarian Association, 1904.

Greenleaf, Moses. *A Survey of the State of Maine: In Reference to its Geographical Features, Statistics and Political Economy.* Portland, ME: Shirley and Hyde, 1829.

Massachusetts General Court, Committee on the Eastern Lands, and Land Agent Office for District of Maine. "Eastern Lands Papers: Records, 1717–1860."

———. Colonial and Early Settlement Materials of Massachusetts Archives Collections. Boston, MA: Secretary of the Commonwealth of Massachusetts, 1717–1860.

Morison, Samuel Eliot. *The Story of Mount Desert Island.* Boston, MA: Little, Brown, 1960.

Morrison, Peter. *Changes on the (Is)land: Baker Island, Acadia National Park, Maine: Archaeological Reconnaissance.* Freeport, ME: Crane & Morrison Archaeology, 2008.

National Archives and Records Administration. United States Light-House Board entries in annual reports concerning Baker Island. Washington, DC: 1853–1905.

National Park Service. *Cultural Landscapes Inventory: Baker Island.* 2009.

Price, Franklin H. *Acadia Maritime Cultural Resources Inventory.* 2008.

Snell, Charles W., ed. *List of Lighthouses, Lighted Beacons, and Floating Lights of the Atlantic, Gulf, and Pacific Coasts of the United States.* U.S. Government Printing Office.

Wasson, Samuel. *A Survey of Hancock County, Maine.* Augusta, ME: Sprague, Owen & Nash, 1878.

Bar Harbor Record, *Mount Desert Herald*, and *Bar Harbor Times* archives, 1882–1962.

Interviews with Calvin Alley, Mildred Chalmers, Paula Richardson Gannon, Henry Grandgent, Leona Gilley Sawyer, George Sawyer Sr., Jennie Sawyer, Kenneth Sawyer, Christopher Speakman, Les Stanley, Ralph W. Stanley, Frances Appleton Wetherell, Myrt Faulkingham White, and Phil Whitney, 1965–2017.

Ralph W. Stanley family letters, 1859–1948.

Lyle Stepanek letters, 1943.

About Keepers of Baker Island

Keepers of Baker Island's mission is to preserve, protect, and promote stewardship of Baker Island's natural and cultural resources for the enjoyment, education, and inspiration of visitors, now and in the future.

Stewardship on Baker has been an important consideration for generations of residents and visitors alike. The seeds of interest in this modern era were planted with the arrival of the Pearson and Kolm families. Another moment of significance occurred after the park authorized residents to cut some trees and place them on existing burn piles. Working with enthusiasm, residents turned a pile into a 200-foot windrow. Late one day, a large tree growing against the tower's fence was carefully cut and wedged away from the buildings. Once felled, the shadow the spruce had cast for decades was clearly visible in the form of accelerated decay of the bricks. This stark demonstration confirmed that more needed to be done for Baker, without delay.

At the suggestion of park management, a nonprofit was formed by residents in 2010, Keepers of Baker Island (KOBI).

Each season, KOBI is thanked repeatedly for making the island look better than it has in years. While KOBI's contribution is significant, support from Acadia National Park, volunteers, and other supporters has been critical in reaching these goals.

KOBI's minimum standard for stewardship on Baker is keeping the island from again sliding backward. To this end, annual maintenance will always be a critical component. Looking ahead, there is a need for further spruce reduction, a challenging, labor-intensive task. As KOBI turns the corner on the fields and forest, focusing on the structures is an obvious next step. The National Park Service's condition assessments and treatment plans spell out minimal next steps with plans for possible further restoration.

KOBI looks forward to continuing its partnership with Acadia and serving as a hub for visitors, locals, and all others who support the care of the island.

MADE IN THE
USA